STRANGELY WARMED

Bob
Morrissey

Strangely Warmed

The Amazing Life of JOHN WESLEY

by Garth Lean

Tyndale House
Publishers, Inc.
Wheaton, Illinois

ACKNOWLEDGMENTS
*Reference is made to several books on
John Wesley and acknowledgment is due
to the appropriate publishers. The names
of these authors and books are in general
given in the text or the Selected
Bibliography.*
G.D.L.

LIBRARY OF CONGRESS CATALOG CARD NUMBER 79-63649
ISBN 0-8423-6662-8, PAPER
COPYRIGHT © 1964 GARTH LEAN
ALL RIGHTS RESERVED
ORIGINALLY PUBLISHED IN ENGLAND WITH TITLE,
JOHN WESLEY, ANGLICAN
AMERICAN EDITION, TYNDALE HOUSE PUBLISHERS, INC.
FIRST PRINTING, NOVEMBER 1979.
PRINTED IN THE UNITED STATES OF AMERICA.

To the memory
of a great American
FRANK BUCHMAN
to whom I owe much
and who, like Wesley
dared to "speak plain"
to Britain and the world

CONTENTS

PREFACE

Britain, after defeating France in the War of the Spanish Succession, was the country of the future. Spain was now in her long decline, and France, though mighty still and yet to be mightier, had been checked. Britain had already gained that almost unchallenged mastery of the seas which was to consolidate her power in America and the West Indies, to win her India and Canada and, in due time, to defeat Napoleon himself. Her commerce and her colonies were growing together and, as the eighteenth century wore on, the quickening Industrial Revolution was to put her a jump ahead of every rival. The nineteenth century, everywhere, would largely be hers to shape. Of what kind and quality would that shaping be?

A nation can only reproduce the quality which is within her, and, at first sight, the self-confident oligarchs who ruled Britain seemed well-placed to give the world a lead. Their ancestors had curbed the power of the Crown and they were evolving a Parliamentary system which was the envy and astonishment of continental observers. Englishmen were free to say and publish what they liked, there was no arbitrary imprisonment or torture, and members of religious sects were allowed to flourish, even if dissenters and Catholics were still, in many ways, treated as second-class citizens. The ruling classes themselves lived singularly stable and pleasant lives in their stout, red-brick houses, and, for any one above the poverty line, it must have seemed that the country had reached a position of assured and inner peace.

This was certainly the impression which intelligent visitors carried away during the early part of the eighteenth century. Voltaire, who arrived in Britain in 1726, fresh from imprisonment without trial for challenging a nobleman, and stayed till 1728, noted the contrast with France: "An Englishman," he wrote, "goes to heaven by the road he pleases. There are no arbitrary taxes. A nobleman or a priest is not exempt from paying certain taxes. The peasant eats white bread and is well clothed, and is not afraid of adding to his hoard for fear that the taxes may be raised next year." Montesquieu, who followed him in 1729, agreed: "England is the freest country in the world. I make no exception of any republic. And I call it free because the sovereign, whose person is controlled and limited, is unable to inflict any imaginable harm on anyone."

Yet, beneath the polished surface which England presented to her visitors, she was less worthy of emulation than at first appeared. "In England the first half of the century was a period of moral disorder," writes Harold Nicolson with the detachment of the intervening two hundred years. "The politicians were corrupt, the ecclesiastics lax, the middle classes intent only on making money, and the masses of the people licentious, drunken and raw." The ruling classes, in particular, were not as different from those of France as was supposed. "The venality of English political life," writes Marlowe, "was the counterpart of the coarseness and profligacy of the social life of the English governing class. And there was a quality about it even more repellent than venality — the quality of heartlessness. There was very little to choose between the political and social morals of the English and the French aristocracy in the century before the French revolution."

Wherever one looks this heartlessness was in evidence. A vital factor in the expanding commerce of the country was the slave trade, whose development every statesman, including Chatham, made a principal object of policy. As the century proceeded, the horrors of the slave ship were matched by the bargeloads of children shipped by parish overseers in London and other large cities to provide the textile factories of the North with cheap labor. A whole theory of economics was produced to convince the nation that such things had to be, that the navy would decay, for instance, without the slave trade, and the economy collapse without child labor.

Heartlessness was, indeed, an inner spirit of the age — for it was on the misery of the many that the calm, cultured life of the few rested. And now, with Britain's gathering power, this spirit might well have become the dominant spirit of the age to come. Had this been so, it might have caused untold suffering. Africa, to take one instance, would have become, in Trevelyan's words, "a slave farm so enormous that it must eventually have corrupted and destroyed Europe herself, as surely as world-conquest under conditions of slavery destroyed the Roman Empire."

A spirit can only be cast out by a stronger spirit. From what source was such a spirit to be initiated? The search for holiness represented by the new religious societies within the Church were signs of a stirring; but they did not, of themselves, go far or deep enough.

Professor H. W. V. Temperley strikes the balance in his brilliant essay in the *Cambridge Modern History*:

The earlier half of the eighteenth century is an age of materialism, a period of dim ideals, of expiring hopes; before the middle of the century its character was transformed. There appeared a movement headed by a mighty leader, who brought water from the rocks to make a barren land live again. . . . No age is without its individual protests and rebels, without men who seek to dam or to direct the stream of tendency. Of these men, Chatham among politicians, Thomson among poets, Berkeley among philosophers, Law among divines, all derived new thoughts, evoked new harmonies, or caught new inspirations from the age. But more important than any of these in universality of influence and in range of achievement was John Wesley. . . .

John Wesley was born in 1703, at Epworth, in the marshy Lincolnshire countryside. His life and work were to change in many respects the very spirit of England — and so to help in shaping the age to come.

ONE
Making of a Man

John Wesley was born on June 17, 1703, in the first year of Queen Anne's reign. The circumstances of his birth tell us much about his parents and his times.

His father, Samuel Wesley, was a High Church Tory, but a King William man. A year before John's birth, he happened to notice that his wife did not say "Amen" to the prayer for King William. He called her to his study and was horrified to discover it was because she regarded James as the true king. "If we have two kings, Sukey, we must have two beds," Samuel cried. He then fell on his knees, and, in Mrs. Wesley's words, "imprecated the divine vengeance upon himself and his posterity if ever he touched me or came into bed with me before I had begged God's pardon."

Mrs. Wesley held her ground, so Samuel left for London, saying he would seek a naval chaplaincy. He left his wife with "6 very little children, which though he tells me he will take good care of, yet if anything should befall him at sea we should be in no very good condition." Toward the end of the summer Samuel came home, intending to stay for a few days before departing for ever. Just then a fire destroyed some part of the rectory — and this effected a reconciliation.

The pregnancy which resulted terminated in the birth of their fifteenth child. So John Wesley was born, the child of an age when politics and religion were entwined and passionate — an age which had seen many of the best of the clergy expelled from their livings for conscience' sake.

His father, Samuel, was a man of principle, vehement and partisan, often pedantic, always brave. Samuel's father and grandfather had both been evicted from their Dorset livings in 1662 for their puritan leanings. He himself had been intended for the nonconformist ministry, but, at Oxford, had moved into the High Church camp. He had, however, kept the pugnacity of his fathers and his usual opponents were his parishioners, admittedly a people not slow to take offense. "Conscientious enough to earn their dislike, but insufficiently gracious to win their affection," he irritated them so much that they stabbed his cattle, maimed his dog, probably set fire to his crops and house, threatened to "squeeze his guts out" and "turn his children out of doors a begging." In 1701 his barn collapsed; in 1702 the rectory was partly burned; in 1703 his flax crop and in 1709 his whole rectory were destroyed by fire. "We have now very little more than what Adam and Eve had when they first set up house-keeping," he wrote to a friend. Yet he would not yield. "Most of my friends advise me to leave Epworth," he wrote to the Archbishop of York in 1705. "I confess I am not of that mind, because I may yet do good there; and 'tis like a coward to desert my post because the enemy fire thick upon me. They have only wounded me yet, and I believe *can't* kill me."

Susanna, his wife, also came from dissenting stock. She was the twenty-fifth child of Dr. Samuel Annesley, who was known as "the Saint Paul of nonconformity." She had characteristically rejected the "stern Calvinism" of nonconformity at the age of thirteen on theological grounds and joined the Church of England. But she had retained the firm piety and inner discipline of her upbringing. She was as masterful as her husband was obstinate — and where he was weak, she was businesslike, practical, and determined. She had need to be. She had never wanted for bread since her marriage, she told the Archbishop of York in 1705, "but, then, I had so much care to get it before it was eat, and to pay for it after, as has often made it very unpleasant for me." She was a handsome woman, who not only taught her children six hours a day, but in the absence of her husband and to the fury of his curate, held prayers for 200 of his parishioners in her kitchen. Her vitality was undimmed by nineteen childbirths. She was fond of her husband, and there was affection in the home; but no one was in any doubt that the stronger personality was Mrs. Wesley.

Samuel found refuge from his cares in his literary work — his output of verse was immense and learned, if unmemorable — and the atmosphere of scholarship which emanated from his study much affected the children. But their upbringing was firmly in his wife's hands. She was well-read herself, valued book-learning, and boasted that none of the children had taken more than a day to learn the alphabet. But her main concern was to raise them to act strictly and honestly.

The vicarage was not a grim place. It was known as "the nest of singing birds" because brothers and sisters were happy, united, and ready rhymers. Visits to local fairs, cards, dancing, and similar amusements were normal there — but the régime was strict, as with so large a family it no doubt had to be. "When turned one year old (and some before)," Mrs. Wesley explained to John in later years, "the children were taught to fear the rod, and to cry softly, by which means they escaped abundance of correction which they might otherwise have had." Her system was built on obedience. "The first thing to be done is to conquer the will and bring about an obedient temper," she wrote. "When a child is corrected, it must be conquered, and this will be no hard matter, if it be not grown headstrong by too much indulgence. And when the will of the child is totally subdued, and it is brought to revere and stand in awe of the parents, then a great many childish follies and inadventures may be passed by." This way provided the "only strong and rational foundation of a religious education," since self-will was the evident root of all sin and misery.

Mrs. Wesley sincerely believed that, by her method, she was training her children to obey God, even if, in the first instance, they were obeying her. And who will say that she was wrong? It has been said that she made so deep an impression on her children that they never shook it off — that the girls, for example, all made unhappy marriages and that John himself could never bring himself to propose marriage because of a "mother-fixation." In fact, the misfortunes of the Wesley daughters seem more often to have been caused by Samuel than Susanna and the slick psychological phrase is a gross oversimplification of John's dealings with women. Be that as it may, it is certain that Susanna marked her children deeply. The code of conduct she taught never left them; the picture of God which she gave them in childhood shaped their conceptions through life. And of none of them is this truer than of John. In particular, he owed to her the discipline of his mind, of which his father remarked so early: "Our Jack would do nothing . . . unless he could give a reason for it."

Susanna felt from very early years that there was something special about John. "Son John," she wrote in her meditation on May 17, 1711, "I do intend to be more particularly careful of the soul of this child than ever I have been: that

I may instil into his mind the principles of true religion and virtue. Lord give me grace to do it sincerely and prudently, and bless my attempts with good success." This feeling had been reinforced by the dramatic events of that February night two years earlier, when parishioners had set fire to the vicarage and burned it to the ground. John, aged five, had been forgotten in the excitement. Wakened by the flames in the thatch above his head, he had dragged a chest to the window, smashed the glass, and called for help. A rescuer stood on another man's shoulders, and John stepped into his arms, just as the roof timbers fell in. Ever afterward his mother called him "the brand plucked from the burning." Perhaps, too, she remembered that other fire without which he might never have been born.

The austerity of a home never far above the poverty line prepared John for Charterhouse, which he entered when he was ten. Bullying was the rule of the day, and the younger boys were forced to become vegetarians, because their elders stole and ate every scrap of their meat. John does not seem to have had unhappy memories of the place, however, and in old age even attributed his marvelous constitution to the bread and water diet on which he existed there. He was a good scholar and at seventeen moved on to Christ Church, Oxford, with a scholarship of forty pounds a year. This still left him poor enough. He wore his hair long because he could not afford to have a wig or have it cut. Describing how a friend had had his cap and wig stolen from him as he stood at a coffeehouse door, he added: "I am pretty safe from such gentlemen; for unless they carried me away, carcass and all, they would have but a poor purchase."

Tyerman, Wesley's classic biographer, wrote: "John Wesley entered the Charterhouse a saint and left it a sinner." He also inferred that John lived an immoral life at Oxford. There is no evidence for either statement. Wesley himself wrote in 1738 shortly after his "conversion" that, during his early years at Oxford, he said his prayers regularly and read the Scriptures, but had no "notion of inward holiness; nay, went on habitually, and for the most part very contentedly, in some or other known sin." Probably he was troubled, at school and Oxford, by some of the usual problems of boyhood. But his judgment of himself was always harsh, and his need seems rather to have been a lack of positive purpose.

"I distinctly remember," he wrote in 1789, "that, even in my childhood, even when I was at school, I have often said: 'They say the life of a schoolboy is the happiest in the world; but I am sure I am not happy; for I am not content, and so cannot be happy.' When I had lived a few years longer, being in the vigour of youth, a stranger to pain and sickness, and particularly to lowness of spirits (which I do not remember to have felt one-quarter of an hour ever since I was born); having plenty of all things, in the midst of sensible and amiable friends, who loved me and I loved them; and being in the way of life which, of all others, suited my inclinations; still I was not happy. I wondered why I was not, and could not imagine what the reason was. The reason certainly was I did not know God: the Source of present as well as eternal happiness."

Such dissatisfaction was well hidden during these first Oxford years. He had gained the reputation of an industrious, keen-witted, and lively student, who reveled in company, and read widely. He was passionately interested in plays — the usual light reading in those days before the novel — but also devoured English literature and the classics, as well as medical and scientific books, with that inquisitive application which later made him "the best gatherer and scatterer of useful knowledge that Georgian England knew." Too frail in health to excel in sport, he yet played tennis, rowed, swam, hunted, and walked long distances with equal zest.

He entered into every discussion with vigor — and sometimes with anger.

His spirit is well illustrated in his encounter with the famous Dr. Sacheverell. "I found him as tall as a maypole and as proud as an archbishop," Wesley told the story years later. "I was a very little fellow. He said, 'You are too young to go to the university. You can know no Greek and Latin yet. Go back to school.' I looked at him as David looked at Goliath and despised him in my heart. I thought, if I do not know Greek and Latin better than you I ought to go back to school indeed. I left him and neither entreaties nor commands would have brought me back to him." "There speaks the real Wesley," comments Arnold Lunn in his absorbing biography of Wesley. "'I looked at him as David looked at Goliath.' It was thus that Wesley looked at the world."

In 1725 John reached a crisis. The time of his ordination was approaching. His father, perhaps sensing some uncertainty in him, was advocating further study, while his mother urged immediate ordination. At the same time, he had begun to visit the Cotswold vicarages of Stanton, Broadway, and Buckland, where he met a bevy of young men and girls — it is of the girls that we hear most — who moved in an easier and more cultivated society than he had known before. All these girls — the three Kirkham sisters, the two Granvilles, and the Griffiths — were interested in serious conversation, especially when conducted by John. They were as delighted to listen to the lively young Oxford man, with his "little, but handsome, person," as he was to address them.

It seems to have been one of the Kirkham sisters who introduced him, in the spring of 1725, to Thomas à Kempis.[1] John was, he says, at first angry with à Kempis for being "too strict." "Yet," he continues, "I had such comfort in reading him, such as I was an utter stranger to before; and meeting likewise with a religious friend, which I never had till now, I began to alter the whole form of my conversation and to set in earnest upon a new life." It was at this time, too, that he "became convinced that there is no medium; but that *every* part of my life (not *some* only) must either be a sacrifice to God, or myself—that is, in effect, to the devil." It was this conviction that led him to fear being a "half Christian"—or the "Almost Christian" of his Oxford University sermon.

John now set aside an hour or two a day for devotional seclusion, took communion every week, watched against all sin, whether in word or deed, and began to aim at, and pray for, inward holiness. "I began to see," he concludes, "that true religion was seated in the heart, and that God's law extended to all our thoughts, as well as to words and actions."

Susanna wrote to him at about this time, noting his "alteration of temper" and recommending a "strict examination" of himself. From now on, there appear in his diary[2] regular records of his shortcomings and of the resolutions with which he tried to meet them. On the eve of his ordination in September 1725, he notes boasting, greed of praise, intemperate sleep, distractions, lying, and heat in arguing as his salient faults. Such lists were to appear frequently in future years, particularly on Saturday evenings when he reviewed the past week, and prepared for the next.

On December 1, 1725, for example, he wrote: "Breach of vows: hence careless of fixing days of mortification, etc.

"Pride of my parts of holiness: greedy of praise: peevishness: idleness.

"Intemperance in sleep: sins of thought: hence useless and sinful anger.

"Breach of promise: dissimulation: lying: rash censures: contemning others: disrespectful of governors: desire to seem better than I am.

"Resolution: to fast every Wednesday in the month."

As the weeks and months went by, John was tempering his life and mind to a firm discipline. He began to rise at six, then five, then four — for he caught himself lying awake in bed and believed that lazing between warm sheets was bad for both spiritual and physical health. Equally, there was discipline in his time of going to bed at night. Dr. Johnson said in later years, "John Wesley's conversation is good, but he is never at leisure. He is always obliged to go at a certain hour. This is very disagreeable to a man who loves to fold his legs and have out his talk, as I do."

"I am full of business, but I have found a way to write without taking any time from that," he noted at this time. "It is but rising an hour sooner in the morning and going into company an hour later in the evening." "Idleness slays" is his constant cry and by idleness he means any lesser use of time. Here was the genesis of his later advice to his preachers: "Never be unemployed for a minute. Never be triflingly employed. Never wile away time."

The one place where John relaxed his regime a little — and could even be said to have wiled away the time — was in those gracious Cotswold vicarages, just a day's ride from Oxford. He took that ride often, sometimes with Charles, sometimes with Robert Kirkham, sometimes alone. There he spent the days walking and riding, singing, reading, dancing, and conversing with the charming young ladies of those households. As the fashion of the day demanded, each of the group took a nickname. John was Cyrus and his brother Araspes; the Kirkham girls were Varanese and Sappho; and the Granville sisters, Aspasia and Selina. When they were parted, frequent letters passed between them.

John — and later Charles — took to these relationships easily and delightfully, as young men who were good company and had been used to a crowd of clever sisters. As might be expected, John's affections soon became involved —

as did those of several of the young ladies. On almost his first visit, he fell more than a little in love with Varanese, who, it now seems clear, was Sally Kirkham.[3] She was already engaged to the local schoolmaster and, in fact, married him in December 1725, having five children and growing increasingly in love with her husband. Yet for several years John's sweet serious dalliance with her continued. Her sisters, Betty and Damaris, also seem to have entertained hopes of John, and he told them he wished to have exactly the same freedom with them as with their sister. Later he was to carry on for a year or more a correspondence as intimate, if less amorous, with Mrs. Pendarves, the elegant young widow among them who was already becoming a light of London society.

All this, innocent enough in itself, began to create an increasing turmoil in John's heart and mind. Always attracted by a pretty woman, provided she was also "serious," he did not yet know when the line of danger was crossed. Throughout life he was apt to idealize women and treat them as far more spiritual than himself, and he did not yet see how he tempted them. "Have I loved women and company more than God?" he asked himself on his return from Varanese's wedding. Yet he went on with it again.

Meanwhile, in March 1726, Wesley had been elected a Fellow of Lincoln, a small college with a reputation for piety and learning rare in the Oxford of that time. His father, who had just found that he had only five pounds to carry his family through the six months to harvest and remembered the debtors' prison, feared for his own future, but exclaimed: "Wherever I am, my Jack is Fellow of Lincoln." John entered into his new duties with zest. He was appointed lecturer in Greek and greatly enjoyed presiding over the daily disputations in logic. By now he also read Hebrew and Arabic, and ranged at large in metaphysics, natural philosophy, divinity, and poetry.

Twice during these years Wesley returned to Lincolnshire to act as his father's curate at the twin parishes of Epworth and Wroote. There, among parishioners whom sister Hetty described as "asses dull on dungheaps born," he visited, shot plovers on the ploughland, wrote sermons for his father and himself, and went to every fair within reach. He also wrote long letters to the young ladies in the Cotswolds, fell a little in love with Miss Kitty Hargreaves, laboriously copied out his father's *Dissertations on Job*, and read mightily, summarizing as he went. Nor was the Saturday evening self-examination neglected.

"What a contrast between the daily life of 1726 and that of 1739," writes the indefatigable editor of his journals. "At Wroote we see a better sort of country parson in times degenerate. He is gentlemanly, refined, familiar with the best literature of the day, a congenial companion; to some extent worldly, yet standing absolutely clear of grossness; not exempt from temptation, but 'buffeting' his body and bringing himself under the iron rule of law and resolution. Could such a man ever have aroused a whole nation to religious enthusiasm?"

Yet even as he sojourned at Wroote, a further step was being prepared for John Wesley. His young brother, Charles, who had lived with their elder brother at Westminster since he was eight and had become Captain of Westminster School, went up to Christ Church in 1726. He was a warm personality and, like all his family, an enthusiastic classic and something of a poet. In his brother's house he had met Pope, Prior, and Swift, and had developed a passion for the stage which included a mild entanglement with a certain Miss Mollie of the Royal Theatre, Lincolns-Inn-Fields. He was a generous and happy-go-lucky boy, rescuing with ready fists a small Scottish boy, the future Chief Justice Mansfield, from his persecutors and preferring poverty at Oxford with

John to the Irish inheritance of a wealthy but childless kins-man which was at this stage offered to him.[4] Naturally such a young man took a full part in the life of the college, and answered John's religious advances with an impatient: "What, would you have me be a saint all at once?"

Then, in January 1729, John at Wroote received a letter from Charles which surprised him. "I verily think that I shall never quarrel with you again till I do with my religion, and that I may never do that I am not ashamed to desire your prayers," wrote Charles. "This owing in great measure to somebody (my mother most likely) that I am come to think as I do, though I can't tell myself how or when I first awoke out of my lethargy — only that 'twas not long after you went away."

Charles gathered two or three men around him. They decided to live, in contrast to the Oxford of the day, a disciplined life, to work hard and read the Greek Testament together. It was their determination to "observe the method of study prescribed in the statutes of the University," Charles said, which earned them "the harmless name of Methodists." Their practice of going to communion each week made others call them "The Sacramentalists," to which still others added "The Bible-Moths" and "The Enthusiasts." John, returning from Wroote in November 1729, was asked to join them and speedily became their leader. With the founding of this "company," as John preferred to call it, John's interest for the first time began to move out from concern for his own spiritual well-being to the care and cure of others.

TWO
Oxford Rehearsal

Oxford, during the first half of the eighteenth century, was in a period of decline. There were, of course, conscientious teachers — Wesley himself in 1726 said he would think himself "little better than a highwayman" if he did not lecture every week day of the term — and names like Blackstone, Kennicott, Hody, and Lowth show that there were some great scholars, as there was great building, in this century. But in general the teaching, inside and outside college, was perfunctory. Most Fellows were not tutors, still less researchers, but rather clergy drawing a salary and waiting for a suitable college living. Amhurst and Gibbon both say that professors seldom or never lectured. Amhurst states roundly, "I have known a profligate debauchee chosen professor of moral philosophy; and a Fellow, who never looked upon the stars soberly in his life, professor of astronomy. We have had history professors who never read anything to qualify them for it but *Tom Thumb, Jack the Giant Killer, Don Beliamis of Greece.* We have likewise numberless professors of Greek, Hebrew and Arabik, who scarce understood their mother tongue." Humphrey Prideaux, a disinterested critic, said only a little earlier that most heads of colleges in Oxford were "such as I could scarce commit a dog to their charge."

The majority of dons were in Anglican orders, but many from no sense of vocation. A Fellowship provided security as well as fair comfort, but it nearly always entailed ordination and celibacy. Some Fellows naturally made use of the facilities offered by the fair ladies of the town, while a few, at least, had less straightforward diversions. Hearne mentions a chaplain who was accused of "sodomitical practices" and "advised to go off from college and forbid reading prayers as chaplain there any more." And in 1739 a Warden was discovered to have made homosexual advances to undergraduates as well as to his butler and barber before he fled the country. A tutor of the college was also implicated, but his accuser, a college servant boy, was forced to withdraw his charge and the tutor was advanced in position.

Dr. V. H. H. Green, until recently Senior Tutor of Wesley's old college, states in his *The Young Mr. Wesley* that the real problem of the University in the first half of the eighteenth century was not its inadequacy as a home of learning and scholarship, nor its failure to educate the young, but the bad press it received as a result of its political and religious standpoint, so much at variance with that of the ruling Whig establishment. "The majority of the dons," he writes, "were not the coarse-grained clerics billowing in their gowns as depicted by the caricaturist; they did not neglect their ministerial duties, were more conscientious as tutors than is often supposed, and took an interest in politics and theology, particularly where the latter had a political connotation. . . . There is nothing in fact to suggest that the eighteenth-century don was a man of more scandalous character than his successors." From so learned an authority, this opinion carries great weight. Yet it does seem that, after all allowances have been made, Oxford in the eighteenth century was a travesty of what a university, staffed by Anglican clergy, could and should be.

It was not to be expected that this Oxford would greet the Wesleys' "company" with enthusiasm. Charles' change had already caused comment in Christ Church and now as the two brothers, William Morgan of Christ Church, and Sally's brother, Robert Kirkham of Merton, met together, a concerted attack developed. "Some of the men of wit in Christ Church," wrote John, "entered the lists against us and, between mirth and anger, made pretty many reflections upon the Sacramentalists, as they were pleased to call us." Then men of Merton launched an attack, naming them "The Holy Club." The complaint was one often to be heard in the next fifty years that "they pretended to be more religious than their neighbors."

Some were frightened away by this treatment. Others were attracted. It came down to a battle for each individual. A young Merton man decided on a new life, and as a symbol of it began to take communion regularly. Whereupon "a gentleman, eminent for learning and well-esteemed for piety" went after him, and after a sustained siege recaptured him. Two other young Merton men were similarly dissuaded, and great was the rejoicing of the "wits." Meanwhile, in Christ Church, a meeting of officers and seniors was summoned to discuss the "new enthusiasm" and it was rumored that the authorities were about to "blow up the Godly Club."

John, meeting persecution for the first time, appealed to his father, who on hearing that John was called the Father of Holy Club, had written: "If it be so, I am sure I must be the Grandfather of it, and I need not say that I had rather any of my sons should be so dignified and distinguished than to have the title of His Holiness." Old Samuel was as brisk as ever. "I can scarcely think so meanly of you as that you would be discouraged with the 'crackling of thorns under a pot,'" he wrote to John. "Preserve an equal temper of mind under whatever treatment you meet with from a not very just or well-natured world. Bear no more sail than is necessary, but steer steady."

The outward issue seems to have been whether one should take communion often, and crowds of undergraduates would gather to jeer as the little company went into Christ Church or St. Mary's. But meanwhile, William Morgan had visited a condemned murderer at the Castle, and taken the Wesleys with him for other visits. Morgan also began to help poor families and to run a school for the prisoners' children. Soon these and other charitable works became standard practice with the company, and the outcry daily increased.

Wesley responded to his critics with a devastating set of questions which began: "Whether it does not concern all men of all conditions to imitate Him, as much as they can, 'who went about doing good'?" "Should they not 'feed the hungry, clothe the naked, visit those who are sick or in prison'?" he continues. "Should they not use method and industry, in order to gather learning or virtue?" Proceeding with inexorable logic, he convinced the openminded, but enraged the unconvincible. In 1732 the first public attack came in a paper aptly named *Fog's Weekly Journal*. In the same year, William Morgan died and John was widely accused of killing him by causing him to undergo undue austerities. So the battle raged.

The year 1732 also saw the arrival of new recruits, among them William Smith, another Fellow of Lincoln, and George Whitefield, the third great name of the Awakening. Men only joined their fortunes with the Wesleys after serious thought, and there were always many more, especially among Wesley's pupils, who were wavering. Tides ebbed and flowed. In 1733 there were twenty-seven regularly taking communion together, but some months later only five re-mained. "One young nobleman" told Wesley he was "more and more afraid of singularity." Another had been detached by "a fever and Dr. Frewin," the Oxford physician. "My ill success, as they call it," John told his father, "seems to be what has frightened everyone away from a falling house."

George Whitefield's story may be taken as typical of many. He had entered Pembroke College in 1732 as a servitor, just as Samuel Johnson left that college. He had heard of the Wesleys while still working at his mother's Bell Inn at Gloucester, and had defended them to other students. When he saw them going to communion at St. Mary's through a ridiculing crowd, he felt "strongly pressed to follow their example," but through fear and diffidence made no contact. Hearing, however, that a woman had tried to commit suicide, Whitefield sent word to Charles Wesley by a "poor aged apple-woman of our college," strictly charging her not to mention his own name. She disobeyed and the result was breakfast with Charles the next morning. "It was one of the most profitable visits I ever made in my life," wrote Whitefield in his journal. "My soul was athirst for some spiritual friends to lift up my hands when they hung down and to strengthen my feeble knees. He soon discovered it, and, like a wise winner of souls, made all his discoveries tend that way. And when he had put into my hand Professor Frank's treatise 'Against the Fear of Man' . . . I took my leave." So started the work of this most eloquent of preachers, a man of warm affection if erratic judgments, who was to stir England and all America.

Meanwhile, there appeared in London a trenchant reply to the attack in *Fog's Journal* which may have been written by the mystic William Law. "It looks," commented the author, "as if the strict Rule of primitive Christianity is removed a great way out of sight, that we are not able to

behold the Attempt to revise it, without wonder and offence." He added a prophecy: "If it shall please God to give
these Gentlemen the grace to persevere, and the Blessing of
so long a Life, they may be the Means of reforming a vicious
world; and may rejoice at the Good they have done, perhaps
Half a Century after most of their Social Opponents, the
gay Scoffers of the present Generation, are laid low and
forgotten, as if they had never Been." A striking prophecy,
amply fulfilled — though it should be noted that of all his
Oxford men only Charles and George Whitefield were con-
spicuous with John in his future enterprise. Most of Wesley's
Oxford men did good work in their country livings. But the
Holy Club is seen in the end to have had significance chiefly
in the development it brought to George Whitefield and the
two Wesleys.

THREE
American Fiasco

On 25 April 1735, old Samuel died as he had lived, bravely, even prophetically — and in debt. "The fear of death he had entirely conquered," wrote Charles to their elder brother, Samuel. "At last he gave up his latest human desires, of finishing *Job*, paying his debts, and seeing you." John and Charles were both present. "O, my Charles, be steady," their father said to his youngest son. "The Christian faith will surely revive in this kingdom; you shall see it though I shall not."

Samuel's debts were computed at 100 pounds. Even while he was "being buried very frugally, yet decently" in the churchyard, one of his parishioners seized "all the quick stock, valued at above £40 for £15 he owed her."

Old Samuel had long foreseen the difficult circumstances in which his death would leave his wife and unmarried daughters. So he had been pressing his sons that one of them should take over the living of Epworth and continue the home. His eldest son, Samuel, had refused, citing his recent appointment as Headmaster of Blundells. Charles was not yet ordained. So the whole weight of family pressure fell on John.

John also had refused, in December 1734, in a letter of prodigious length, in which he argued that he must stay in Oxford because there "I can most promote holiness in myself." He had added: "I know no other place under heaven where I can have always at hand half a dozen persons nearly of my own judgment and engaged in the same studies: persons who were awakened into a full and lively conviction that they only have one work to do upon earth, who have according to their power renounced themselves and wholly and absolutely devoted themselves to God."

This letter, writes Green, was "an appalling piece of self-indictment." "The unreadiness to step outside the circle of the select and self-appointed Christian group, the general air of smugness and even of self-satisfaction . . . leave an unpleasing taste. If Wesley really wanted the life of self-denial and contempt, the bearing of the Cross, all the things which he stressed so much, then the parish of Epworth provided them as richly as did Oxford." Certainly the letter, with its twenty-six points, reveals a self-concern and a desire to justify himself which seems far from the Spirit. But Green seems here to miss the point. Wesley was a man of strong vocation, unsure what his next step should be. But he *was* sure that the comfortable little world of Epworth and Wroote, the family circle, the garden and neighborly visits, which he had twice enjoyed, was not the life God wanted for him. At the same time it was hard to refuse, in the face of his father's failing health and his mother's need. Nor was it made easier when brother Samuel shrewdly appealed to his sense of legalistic duty by stating that John was not fulfilling his ordination vows while simply teaching — a strange argument indeed for the Reverend Headmaster of Blundells, but one which sent John once more into a lather of self-examination.

What has puzzled people is that John Wesley decided to

go to Georgia so soon after insisting that he must at all costs stay in Oxford. Wesley did not see this as a contrast. "My chief motive to which all the rest are subordinate is the hope of saving my own soul," he said. "I hope to learn the true sense of the Gospel of Christ by preaching it to the heathen." In a revealing passage he adds, "Toward mortifying the desire of the flesh, the desire of sensual pleasures, it will be no small thing to be able, without fear of giving offence, to live on water and the fruits of the earth. This simplicity of food will, I trust, be a blessed means, both of preventing my seeking that happiness in meats and drinks which God designed should be found only in faith and love and joy in the Holy Ghost; and will assist me — especially where I see no woman but those who are almost of a different species from me — to attain such purity of thought as suits a candidate for that state wherein they neither marry nor are given in marriage. . . . Neither is it a small thing to be delivered from so many occasions as now surround me, of indulging the desire of the eye. They here compass me in on every side: but an Indian hut affords no food for curiosity, no gratification of the desire of grand or new or pretty things."

The fact is that the invitation to go to Georgia presented Wesley with both a challenge and an escape. He saw it as the path to greater holiness, but also he welcomed the escape from an Oxford from which many of his close friends were now scattered into country parishes. He also welcomed the chance to break out of the sweet network of relationships with the young ladies of the Cotswolds, which he now increasingly felt to be hindering him from his life work. Also there was a certain and typical caution in the move. Going to Georgia, radical step though it seemed, did not involve him in resigning his Fellowship at Lincoln, whereas taking the living of Epworth would have done. Wesley, while uncertain where his path would lead, felt he should retain this secure base of operations — and events were to prove him right in this.

Charles seems to have gone to Georgia for an even simpler reason: because John wished it. For by now John had taken the place of Samuel as the dominant influence in Charles' life. "I took my degree, and only thought of spending all my days in Oxford," wrote Charles in his brooding old age. "But my brother, who always had the ascendant over me, persuaded me to accompany him and Mr. Oglethorpe to Georgia." Brother Samuel wrote at the time: "John knew his strength and used it. His will was strong enough to bend you to go, though not me to consent. I freely own 'twas the will of Jack, but am not yet convinced 'twas the will of God."

Charles went to Georgia as Oglethorpe's secretary. Oglethorpe had long been a family friend, much admired by old Samuel to whose poems he subscribed. The Vicar of Epworth had suggested many people for the expedition, but not his sons. It was, however, while John was in London arranging the posthumous publication of his father's *Job* that he met Oglethorpe and agreed to go. Susanna rose to the challenge with characteristic courage: "Had I twenty sons I should rejoice if they were all so employed," she said.

General Oglethorpe was an impressive personality. "The finest figure ever seen, heroic, romantic, full of old gallantry," was Hannah More's description. After a daring military career — Marlborough had made him A.D.C. to Prince Eugene — he had entered the House of Commons and persuaded Parliament to reform the notorious "debtors' prison" system. To give an outlet for these debtors, as well as to block the Spanish expansion north from Florida, he had founded in 1732 the colony of Georgia. Now he was sailing with five hundred and seventy new settlers. He was quite sure that the Wesleys, who had in turn brought Ingham and Delamotte from Oxford, were just the men to care for the spiritual needs of this rough company.

They embarked on October 14, 1735, but it was not until December that the *Simmonds* finally set sail out of Cowes Roads. Among the settlers on board were twenty-six German Moravians under the leadership of their bishop, David Nitschmann. It was at their hands that Wesley was to receive the first lesson of this momentous voyage, momentous not for what Wesley did for the New World, but for what God began to do for Wesley.

In mid-Atlantic, great storms hit the little ship. Wesley was afraid, and disturbed by being afraid. By January 23, he was asking himself: "Why is it that you have no faith?" This was driven home to him by the evident faith of the Moravians. He had noticed that in contrast to the Englishmen aboard, they were ready to do the most menial tasks, never complained when struck or pushed and showed "great seriousness." Were they, he asked himself, delivered from fear, as well as from pride, anger, and revenge? He noted on January 25: "In the midst of the psalm wherewith their service began, the sea broke over, split the main sail in pieces, covered the ship and poured in between the decks, as if the great deep had already swallowed us up. A terrible screaming began among the English. The Germans calmly sang on. I asked one of them afterwards, 'Was you not afraid?' He answered, 'I thank God, no.' I asked, 'But were not your women and children afraid?' He replied mildly, 'No: our women and children are not afraid to die.'"

The demeanor of the Moravians shook John. A day after landing in America, he met Mr. Spangenberg, one of their leading pastors. "I asked Mr. Spangenberg's advice," he wrote in his journal, "with regard to myself — to my own conduct. He said to me, 'Do you know Jesus Christ?' I paused and said, 'I know He is the Saviour of the world.' 'True,' replied he, 'but do you know that He has saved you?' I answered, 'I hope He has died to save me.' He only added, 'Do you know yourself?' I said, 'I do.' But I fear they were vain words." Spangenberg noted in his diary, which has recently been discovered, "I noticed that true grace dwelt and reigned in him."

Once in Georgia John found that he had little to do with the Indians of his imagination, but was parish priest to an extremely hard-boiled set of adventurers and jail birds. He attempted to apply to their moral lapses the penitential disciplines of the early Church. They resented it. And soon it became clear that the method of the Holy Club lacked the dynamic necessary to affect hard-bitten men and women of the world. Instead, the Wesleys were used by intriguers who wished to vilify Oglethorpe. A Mrs. Hawkins and a Mrs. Welch each made to Charles a bogus confession of adultery with Oglethorpe — and then denounced Charles as the originator of the story. This served the double purpose of blackening Oglethorpe and checking the influence of the strict and sober Oxford men upon the General. It was shortly after this incident that Oglethorpe sent his unhappy secretary home with dispatches and the suggestion that he would do well to marry.

John remained. The crisis of his time there focused around his relationship with Sophie Hopkey. Sophie was a pretty, if commonplace, girl of eighteen, the niece of the chief magistrate of Savannah, a man who had cheated the revenue in England, now ran the largest store in town, and was soon to be dismissed from his public appointments for fraud. The uncle certainly saw John as a more eligible match than the two local suitors already at Sophie's door, and Sophie herself was more dazzled than the fair ladies of the Cotswolds. She used to walk over to Wesley's wooden parsonage, alone or with a friend, each morning for early prayers. Wesley also taught her French. Sometimes Delamotte was present; some-times they spoke alone. Wesley became fascinated with her, but went on meeting her long after it was dangerous to do so, partly because he thought that he was Sophie's only hope of salvation and partly because he could not bear to break the relationship.

Wesley made statements both to Sophie and to her relatives which, in anyone else, would have predicted a proposal of marriage. Certainly he considered it and consulted his friends. The Moravians were ambiguous and Oglethorpe sent the pair off on a six-day boat journey together, alone with a small crew. Delamotte was decisively against it — and Wesley's own searching of God's purposes inclined him to the same opinion. He decided passively to await the outcome, but meanwhile went on seeing her. It was desperately hard for him, but even harder for Sophie. Probably he was only saved from a disastrous marriage by his old trick of idealizing women, so that he believed her when she declared that she would never marry.

In the end the uncertainty was too much for Sophie. After giving Wesley every chance and encouragement to speak, she became suddenly engaged to a Mr. Williamson. Wesley was half relieved, wholly incredulous, and greatly hurt. Only in the hour of loss did he perceive how much he wanted her. He soon found that she was abandoning the religious practices she had started under his influence. He solemnly rebuked her, and finally refused her communion publicly. Her husband and uncle then took legal action against him, and after withstanding one trial, he left Georgia for England suddenly, in the night.

Small wonder that Wesley felt dejected as he sailed for England. On January 2, 1738, he noted "being sorrowful and very heavy, though I could give no particular reason for it, and utterly unwilling to speak close to any of my little flock (about twenty persons), I was in doubt whether my neglect of them was not one cause of my own heaviness. In the evening therefore I began instructing the cabin boy: after which I was much easier." Yet the depression persisted: "I have no heart, no vigour, no zeal in obeying: continually doubting whether I was right or wrong," he noted on landing at Deal. "I could do nothing for four days."

He immediately tried to apply a new dose of determination: "I now renewed and wrote my former resolutions." Yet this dejection was to be the prelude to the great experience of his life. For on his return to London he almost immediately met Peter Bohler, a twenty-six-year-old Moravian there on his way to Carolina.

John's first interview with Bohler was on February 7, and from then until May 4, when Bohler left for Carolina, they were often together. "My brother, my brother," the graduate of Jena said to the Oxford don, "that philosophy of yours must be purged away." Wesley was mystified but willing to learn. He asked Bohler whether, being without faith, he should give up preaching. "By no means. Preach faith till you have it; and then, because you have it, you will preach faith," said Bohler. And on March 4 Wesley did so. Bohler's diagnosis of the Wesley brothers is told in a letter to the Moravian leader, Count Zinzendorf, at this time:

"I travelled with the two brothers, John and Charles Wesley, from London to Oxford. The elder, John, is a good-natured man: he knew he did not properly believe on the Saviour and was willing to be taught. His brother is at present very much distressed in mind, but does not know how he will begin to be acquainted with the Saviour. Our mode of believing in the Saviour is so easy to Englishmen that they cannot reconcile themselves to it; if it were a little more artful, they would much sooner find their way in it. Of faith in Jesus they have no other idea than the generality of people have. They justify themselves; and, therefore, they always take it for granted that they believe already, and try to prove their faith by their works, and thus so plague and torment themselves that they are at heart very miserable."

John Wesley describes his battle with Bohler in clear terms: "Peter Bohler affirmed of true faith in Christ that it had those two fruits inseparably attending it, 'dominion over sin and constant peace, arising from a sense of forgiveness.' I was quite amazed and looked upon it as a new gospel. If this was so it was clear that I had no faith, but I was not willing to be convinced of this." Wesley fought with all his strength to prove there might be faith without these two fruits, particularly without the second. Bohler referred him to the Bible and to experience. Consulting the Bible, Wesley became convinced that Bohler was right and was driven back to his last hold: "that experience would never agree with this literal interpretation of the Scriptures." Bohler won the point by producing three friends who affirmed these fruits to be their own experience.

Bohler then contended that this saving faith is given in a moment of time. Again the Bible and experience were consulted. Again Wesley was forced, against all his previous views, to agree.

"I was now thoroughly convinced," said Wesley, "and by the grace of God I resolved to seek it unto the end. (1) By absolutely renouncing all dependence in whole or in part upon my own works or righteousness on which I had really grounded my faith and salvation, though I knew it not, from my youth up. (2) By adding to the constant use of all other means of grace, continual prayer for this very thing, justifying saving faith, a full reliance on the blood of Christ shed for me, a trust in Him as my Christ, as my sole justification, sanctification and redemption."

Meanwhile Charles was fighting a similar battle. Taken

ill in Oxford and again in London, he was attended by Bohler who asked him: "Do you hope to be saved?" When Charles said: "Yes, because I have used my best endeavours to serve God," Bohler simply shook his head. The battle raged in Charles for almost a month, until on Whitsunday night, May 21, 1738, the wonder happened. "I saw," wrote Charles in his journal, "that by Faith I stood."

John still lingered. Then on Wednesday, May 24, he awoke and opened his Bible at the text, "Whereby are given unto us exceeding great and precious promises, that by these ye might be partakers of the divine nature." That morning he went to St. Paul's, and in the evening, very unwillingly, to a society in Aldersgate Street, where someone read Luther's preface to the Epistle to the Romans. "About a quarter before nine, while he was describing the change which God works in the heart through faith in Christ," Wesley relates, "I felt my heart strangely warmed. I felt I did trust in Christ, Christ alone, for salvation: and an assurance was given me that He had taken away my sins, even mine, and saved me from the law of sin and death."

Charles was sitting alone in his lodgings that evening, when a troop of friends bore John to him in triumph, declaring, "I believe." They sang together the exultant lyric which Charles had just composed:

> Where shall my wondering soul begin?
> How shall I all to heaven aspire?
> A slave redeemed from death and sin
> A branch pluck'd from eternal fire.
> How shall I equal triumphs raise,
> Or sing my great Deliverer's praise?

Immediately turning from himself to others, Charles' hymn proceeds:

Outcasts of men, to you I call,
Harlots, and publicans, and thieves!
He spreads His arms to embrace you all:
Sinners alone His grace receives;
No need of Him the righteous have;
He came the lost to seek and save.

The brothers had started on a new road.

FOUR
Destiny Accepted

What really happened to John Wesley in that room at Aldersgate? How important was it for his life work?

The Roman Catholic writer, Piette, considers that Wesley's conversion really dates from his ordination in 1725. In one sense he is right, for Wesley's change began in the decisions he made at that time. It was then that he turned around and began to move in a new direction. Without that turn he would never have got where he did. Yet, as we have seen, it was not for another thirteen years that he crossed the starting line of the real race.

Dr. Green also emphasizes the continuity in Wesley's life. Aldersgate, he says, "made little apparent difference to his theological thinking or to his manner of life." It was "a crisis of a major order from which Wesley emerged in some sense a changed man, though the characteristic features of his personality were the same as they had previously been." He says what Wesley's conversion provided was "a psychological reassurance." "His confidence and faith in the truth of what he was preaching gave him such strength, such dynamic impetus, that he could now move forward into the life of evangelism which took him in the next half-century to every corner of the British Isles."

While it is true that Wesley's basic characteristics remained constant — such characteristics are generally heightened or redirected rather than obliterated by conversion — the words "psychological reassurance" seem strangely inadequate to describe the effect on Wesley. For Bready is unquestionably right when he says in his massive study that if Wesley had died in his thirty-fifth year he would have been "an unremembered man — capable, methodical, hard-working, but pedantic, legalistic, irascible; unloved and well-nigh unlovable." "The most charitable tribute that could then have been paid him," adds Bready, "would have been that he was a sincere, a selfless, almost an heroic failure."

The contrast between the effect of the Wesleys' work before and after 1738, writes Brailsford, "is as extreme as that which is visible in the lives of the Apostles before and after Pentecost." "Before 1738, their sermons were as carefully prepared, and their works of charity even more abundant; their self-denial was as complete and their timetable even more meticulously ordered. But the motive-power of their actions and their impact upon others were as far removed as winter from summer from those that characterized the later period."

Another Roman Catholic writer, John Todd, in a stimulating book, may get nearer the heart of the matter. He sees Wesley's progress as continuous indeed, but of greater depth and significance. He believes that Wesley, in the years since 1725, was undergoing the classic experience described by St. John of the Cross. "When a Christian begins to grasp the need to seek God with his whole being," writes Todd, "he begins also to understand the necessity of mortifying his senses, in order to keep his whole attention on God. He institutes of his own free will — that is, 'actively' — a 'night'

43

of the senses. There will follow a passive night when God takes over; the Christian, having prepared himself by active voluntary mortification, begins to suffer uncovenanted, unexpected, undeserved, inexplicable mortification of his senses."

It was this stage, according to Todd, which Wesley reached in Georgia: "His inner experience at this time can be indicated by saying that the immediate master was no longer himself but God. . . . From the consolations of the palpable goodness of his companions at Oxford, of his own devotions, acts of charity and mortifications, he moved into a period of growing bewilderment. . . . This is the classic sign of the passive night, . . . the essence of the experience is the disappearance of one's own activity in favour of God's activity, an activity, moreover, which comes in unaccustomed ways, not easily understood, involving a certain desolation."

Whatever the truth of Todd's interpretation, it is clear that the experience at Aldersgate marked the transference of the control of Wesley's life from himself to God. No longer does he conduct — and record in his journal — those ceremonies of intense and minute introspection. No longer, when he has a difficult decision to make, does he write a letter of twenty-six points, arguing the pros and cons. His energies were released and directed toward other men still in need of the liberation he had himself received. A bounding joy, absent for so long from his religion, returns. The sense of humor, which was the best gift left to him by old Samuel, breaks dryly through. From now on, his goal is to turn the tide of his age back to God, and he is always seeking for God's way, not his own, of achieving it. The Holy Spirit has become the dynamic force of his life.

Within fifteen months John Wesley had become the focal point of one of the greatest awakenings in British history. And it took place through a series of events which he did not plan and a series of decisions which he did not desire. Summing up his career in later life, he said that he had been "insensibly led without previous plan or design." The secret was that this most reasonable of men was now ready to yield himself to such leading.

His first problem was how to reach the people, and particularly the toiling masses who were "untouched and seemingly untouchable by the Church of England." Wesley had begun by preaching in those churches which invited him. On the Sunday following the Aldersgate experience, he preached at St. George's, Bloomsbury, and at the chapel in Long Acre. The journal adds: "The last time, I understand, I am to preach at either." This became a frequent experience for him, for comfortable Christians now felt in him the "enthusiasm" which they hated most. By the end of 1738 virtually all churches were closed to him. In the whole of 1739 he was only allowed to preach in seven of them. He occupied his time in speaking in prisons and workhouses, in addressing groups who spontaneously came together in private houses, and in personal work with the poor and the outcast. He was happy in this work, but the Spirit could not permanently be so confined.

Meanwhile, George Whitefield, newly returned from his successful mission to America, had been more fortunate. In the first five weeks of 1739 he had preached over thirty sermons in churches in and around London. In February he left for Bristol. But owing to a fracas the previous Sunday at St. Margaret's, Westminster, which must have been reported or misreported to the authorities in Bristol, he was refused admittance to the churches there. On February 17, however, he went to Kingswood, near Bristol, and there preached in the open air to two hundred colliers, men commonly regarded by church and society as more savage than wild beasts. At the second Kingswood meeting he spoke to two thousand people; at the third to four thousand; at the fourth to ten thousand — tremendous crowds to gather out of doors in the bleak months of February and March. Soon he was repeating the performance in Bath and in Cardiff, returning in late March to Bristol where a gentleman lent him a large bowling green in the heart of the city. There he preached to seven or eight thousand people. As he himself had to go to London and then to America, Whitefield called upon John Wesley to fill his place at Kingswood and Bristol. Wesley arrived there on March 31, and next day heard Whitefield at the bowling green.

Whitefield's outdoor method was a great shock to Wesley. "I could scarce reconcile myself at first to this strange way of preaching in the fields of which he had set me an example on Sunday: having been all my life (till very lately) so tenacious to every point relating to decency and order that I thought the saving of souls almost a sin, if it had not been done in a church," wrote Wesley in his diary. However, he sought guidance and examined Whitefield's way by the Scriptures. "The Sermon on the Mount is one pretty remarkable precedent of field preaching," he commented that evening, "though I suppose there were churches at that time also." Less than twenty-four hours later Wesley himself embarked on the new venture.

"At four in the afternoon," he says, "I submitted to be more vile and proclaimed in the highways the glad tidings of salvation, speaking from a little eminence in a ground adjoining the city to about three thousand people." His text for this, the first of many thousand field sermons to come, was: "The Spirit of the Lord is upon me because He hath anointed me to preach the Gospel to the poor; He hath sent me to heal the broken-hearted; to preach deliverance to the captives and recovery of sight to the blind; to set at liberty them that are bruised, to proclaim the acceptable year of the

Lord." For him the Rubicon had been crossed. He had found his way to the people. "From that day, 2 April, 1739," writes Professor Temperley, "may be reckoned a new era in the religious history of England."

Soon another issue was to arise which was to cost Wesley's former principles just as dearly in the deciding. In June 1739, a layman, John Cennick, was called to Kingswood to be the first headmaster of the new school there. When he arrived, he was faced with five hundred miners who had assembled to hear a young man read a sermon to them. But neither the young man nor the text of the sermon was there, and Cennick, after much hesitation, was persuaded to preach himself. This, for a layman, was a startling innovation. Wesley, returning from London, found Cennick and the Welsh layman, Howel Harris, at Kingswood together. The three men took to prayer. Many urged Wesley to forbid them to preach. Whitefield felt that Harris, having three times offered himself for ordination, should be encouraged, but Cennick discouraged. Wesley, however, let him be.

But this was only an individual case. The principle was not settled in Wesley's mind. In the spring of 1740 he heard that Thomas Maxfield, one of the earliest Bristol converts, who had traveled with brother Charles for a time, had begun to preach at Wesley's London headquarters, the Foundry. Wesley, hearing of it in Bristol, hurried back to London to stop him, but Susanna Wesley, who lived in a house adjoining the Foundry, intervened. "John," she said, "take care what you do with respect to that young man, for he is as surely called of God to preach as you are. Examine what have been the fruits of his preaching, and hear him yourself." Wesley listened to his mother, to Maxfield, and was convinced. "It is the Lord's doing," he said. "What am I that I should oppose God?"

A third trial for Wesley centered around the extraordinary

scenes which accompanied his early preaching in Bristol. People began to fall down as though dead, to be convulsed, or to shout aloud. Such scenes were profoundly distasteful to Wesley, the neat little Oxford scholar, so reasonable, ordered, and polished. They were against all his training and convictions. Yet he noticed that, after prayer, such people emerged without harm and that "very many persons changed, in a moment, from the spirit of fear, horror, despair to the spirit of love, joy and peace." So, while keeping a lookout for fakes, Wesley decided neither to encourage nor discourage them. He regarded it as the work of God — or of the Devil counterfeiting Him. "From this time, I trust, we shall all suffer God to carry on His own work in the way that pleaseth Him," he commented. It is undeniable that, while the great majority of Wesley's people never went through such experiences, some of his most consistent men like Pawson and Haine first came to God in this way.[1]

Such willingness to seek out the untrodden ways of God led to much criticism from those set in accustomed ways. Thus the Archbishop of Armagh, a fairer man than most, said one day to Charles Wesley, "I knew your brother well; I could never credit all I heard respecting him and you: but one thing in your conduct I could never account for, your employing laymen."

"My Lord," said Charles, "the fault is yours and your brethren's."

"How so?" asked the Primate.

"Because you hold your peace and the stones cry out."

"But I am told," the Archbishop continued, "that they are unlearned men."

"Some are," answered Charles, "and so the dumb ass rebukes the prophet."

John had a similar encounter, in 1739, with the famous Bishop Butler of Bristol, who had published his celebrated

Analogy of Religion in 1736 and had just arrived in Bristol in time to see Wesley's emergence as a field preacher. The meeting was dramatic for, as Sir John Marriott writes, "These two redeemed the England of the eighteenth century: the one from intellectual unbelief; the other from spiritual apathy and moral degradation." The scholarly Bishop, who had devoted much of his life to the intellectual war against the Deists, was face to face with a man who was reaching the masses who had never read *The Analogy* and perhaps never even heard of its distinguished author.

Butler was one of the more conspicuously pious church-men of the period. But his prim jealous orthodoxy rebelled at field-teaching to the colliers of Kingswood, even though the miners had no parish church within three miles. He comfortably ignored the fact that the growing industrial working class population was indifferent to, or even excluded from, the Church, and held that the ordinary church service, properly conducted, was all that Britain needed.

"You have no business here," Butler told Wesley, after a tart debate. "You are not commissioned to preach in this diocese. Therefore, I advise you to go hence."

Wesley had his answer ready. He pointed out, with more logic than legality, that as he had been ordained not to a parish but as Fellow of Lincoln, he held an indeterminate commission to preach anywhere in the Church of England. "I cannot conceive therefore," he continued, "that in preach-ing here by this commission I break any human law. When I am convinced I do, then it will be time to ask, shall I obey God or man? But if I should be convinced in the meanwhile that I could advance the glory of God and the salvation of souls in any other place, more than in Bristol, in that hour, by God's help, I will go hence; which till then I may not do."

The issue of obeying God or man, and of doing the un-

49

conventional or the conventional, was now at the front of his mind. To some friends who, in 1739, urged him to settle in college again or accept a parish, he said: "I have no business at college, having now no office and no pupils; and it will be time enough to consider whether I ought to accept a cure of souls when one is offered to me. On scriptural grounds, I do not think it hard to justify what I am doing. God, in Scripture, commands me, according to my power, to instruct the ignorant, reform the wicked, confirm the virtuous. Man forbids me to do this in another's parish; that is, in effect, not to do it at all, seeing now I have no parish of my own, nor probably ever shall. Whom then shall I hear? God or man? If it be just to obey man rather than God, judge ye. I look upon all the world as my parish."

"We believe the design of God in raising up the preachers called Methodists," he was to write years later, "is to reform the nation." He did not fully see this as he spoke to Butler. But perhaps he remembered what Lady Huntingdon had said to him some weeks before: "Attempt nothing less than all mankind. The work is nothing to our Lord. We are but just entering upon infinity."

FIVE
Plain Speech on the Road

Wesley's life now swiftly fell into the pattern which was to mark it for the next fifty-two years. He invariably rose at four, and usually preached at five A.M. so that working men could attend before their day's work started. Often, indeed, people would gather to hear him in the evening as he arrived at a place and then would sleep the night in the open or in a public hall nearby, so as to be sure not to miss him in the morning. For after the five o'clock sermon he would mount his horse and ride on to the next place, stopping perhaps in the market place and singing the 100th Psalm until a crowd had gathered. In later years he always preached by appoint-ment, his schedules carefully worked out weeks beforehand. As he stopped in village or country town, the whole popu-lation would often gather to hear this man, the only celebrity ever to visit them.

During those fifty years he traveled 225,000 miles, mostly on horseback, and preached 50,000 sermons in halls, in churches — once even in a Roman Catholic church near Durham — at fairs, in military camps, or in open spaces, wherever he could gain a hearing. As he rode, he would read philosophy, poetry, and history. He once said that never in 100,000 miles of riding had he known a horse stumble as he read, a fact which he attributed to throwing the reins loosely over the horse's neck. He was less fortunate when he was not reading. In 1749 alone he fell head over heels three times, once narrowly escaping death. In July 1743 one horse lay down and died, while in August another threw him and itself ran back to Smithfield. In October of the same year, when he was crossing the River Trent in a ferry boat, a violent storm hurled three horses and eight men all over each other with Wesley at the bottom, pinned down by a large iron bar, utterly unable to move. Generally he escaped injury, though one of his two accidents while reading — that of 1764 — caused him serious damage. Miss Mary Lewen then put a chaise and pair at his disposal, and from that time he generally traveled in a lumbering carriage, with a bookshelf built into it. Yet in 1774 he was still riding through the cold March season and in general he maintained: "I must ride horseback, if I would be healthy."

His determination, faith, and care of men is well illustrated in a story told by Peter Martin of Helston. "One day when I was ostler at the London Inn, Helston," he said, "Mr. Wesley came and obtained my master's leave for me to drive him to St. Ives. On arriving at Hayle, we found the sands between that place and St. Ives, overflown by the rising tide. Mr. Wesley was resolved to go on; for he said he had to preach at St. Ives at a certain hour and must be there. Looking out of the carriage window, he called, 'Take the sea, take the sea.' In a moment I dashed into the waves and was quickly involved in a world of water. The horses were swimming, and the wheels of the carriage not infrequently sunk into the deep hollows in the sand. I expected every moment to be drowned, but heard Mr. Wesley's voice and saw his long white hair dripping with salt water.

" 'What is your name, driver?' he calmly asked.

"I answered, 'Peter.'

" 'Peter,' said he, 'Peter, fear not, thou shalt not sink.'

"With vigorous whipping I again urged on the flagging horses and at last got safely over. Mr. Wesley's first care was to see me comfortably lodged at the tavern; and then, totally unmindful of himself, and drenched as he was with the dashing waves, he proceeded to the chapel and preached according to his appointment."

How did he preach? "In the pulpit," said Tyerman, "Wesley's attitude was graceful and easy; his action calm, natural, pleasing and expressive; and his voice not loud but clear and manly." He used to tell his preachers to speak with emphasis, but never to scream. He also disliked the "luscious" and "amorous" way of preaching. "If we only join faith and works in all our preaching," he wrote to his brother Charles in 1772, "we shall not fail of a blessing. But of all preaching, what is usually called gospel preaching is most useless, if not the most mischievous: a dull, yea, or lively harangue on the sufferings of Christ or salvation by faith, without strongly inculcating holiness. I see, more and more, that this naturally tends to drive holiness out of the world."

He was not dramatically eloquent like George Whitefield, whose description of a blind man tottering toward the crumbling edge of the precipice of sin could bring the urbane Lord Chesterfield to his feet crying, "By God! He's over!" Nor had his voice the melody which made Garrick say that he'd give a thousand guineas to be able to say the single word "Oh!" like Mr. Whitefield. But he would, no doubt, have stood up to the test of the ship builder who said: "Every Sunday that I go to my parish church I can build a ship from stem to stern under the sermon; but, to save my soul, under Mr. Whitefield, I can't lay a single plank." Indeed, when floors subsided while Wesley preached, the congregation listened on "hardly altering their posture." Wesley compelled attention, but by different means than those of Whitefield.

John Nelson, the Yorkshire stonemason who became one of the principal warriors of the awakening, heard Whitefield and Wesley on successive days in the summer of 1739, when they were drawing crowds of up to 80,000 in London, among them many of the rich and powerful. Nelson compared Whitefield to "a man who can play well upon an instrument," and vowed that he would fight anyone who tried to create a disturbance. Of Wesley he wrote: "As soon as he got up on the stand, he stroked back his hair and turned his face towards where I stood and I thought he fixed his eyes on me. His countenance struck such an awful dread upon me before I heard him speak, that it made my heart beat like the pendulum of a clock; and when he did speak, I thought his whole discourse was aimed at me." "Whitefield," comments Vulliamy, "produced the impersonal effect of genius. But Wesley stroked back his hair, looked into your eyes, and you had the sense of being directly apprehended by the mind of the preacher. . . . The power of Whitefield lay in word and gesture, in vigour of delivery, often in coarse language: the power of Wesley was of a more penetrating, spiritual kind."

Wesley's preaching was always searching, but seldom terrible or severe, except when addressed to rich and complacent audiences. "Sir," said a friend to him after he had preached to a genteel congregation from the text: "Ye serpents, ye generation of vipers, how can ye escape the damnation of hell?" "Sir," said Wesley's offended hearer, "such a sermon would have been suitable to Billingsgate; but it was highly improper here." "If I had been in Billingsgate," replied Wesley, "my text should have been, 'Behold the Lamb of God which taketh away the sin of the world.'"

The word which Wesley himself used most often about

his preaching was "plain." "I spoke with all plainness," he writes many times in his journal. By this he meant plainness both of manner and content—but above all a plain application to his hearers. He was fearless as to reaction. Of two sermons preached on a single Sunday he noted, "The second was the most blessed, as it gave the most offence."

Wesley's courage is well illustrated by the sermon which he delivered before the University of Oxford on August 24, 1744. He was devoted to Oxford. "I love the very sight of Oxford," he said in old age. "I love its manner of life; I love and esteem many of its institutions." Also he owed Oxford a great deal, for it was his Fellowship at Lincoln which gave him a slight financial independence, while it was his ordination as a Fellow of a College which gave him license to officiate throughout the kingdom, and not just in one parish. So, on that August day when he mounted the pulpit in St. Mary's and faced the Vice-Chancellor, the Heads of Houses, and many of those he had known as Fellows, he might well have spoken less than plainly through human affection, financial fear, or knowledge of that freezing chill which Oxford disapproval can bring. Or, since he had been attacked directly and indirectly many times from that pulpit in the previous six years, he might have been anxious to defend himself. Wesley took none of these courses.

He began with a description of the activity and influence of the Holy Spirit in the early church. He continued by considering the growth of Christianity and drew the picture of a Christian community in which the Holy Spirit was actively at work. This occupied two-thirds of his sermon and so far a large audience—many of the Heads of Houses standing throughout—was attentive and unruffled.

"Having thus briefly considered Christianity as beginning, as going on and as covering the earth," Wesley continued, "it remains only that I should close the whole with a plain, practical application. I beseech you, brethren, by the mercies of God, if you do account me a madman or fool, yet as a fool bear with me. It is utterly needful that someone should use great plainness of speech towards you. And who will use this plainness, if I do not? Therefore I will speak.

"Let me ask you then, in tender love, and in the spirit of meekness, Is this city a Christian city?" he began. "Are we, considered as a community of men, so 'filled with the Holy Ghost' as to enjoy in our hearts and show forth in our lives the genuine fruit of that spirit? Are all the magistrates, heads and governors of colleges and halls, and their respective societies of one heart and one soul? Is the love of God shed abroad in our hearts? Are our tempers the same that were in Christ? And are our lives agreeable thereto?"

His audience became restive as by a series of devastating questions he showed only too clearly that the rulers of Oxford were not obvious channels of the Holy Spirit. "I pray you that are in authority over us, whom I reverence for your office' sake, consider, Are you filled with the Holy Ghost? Are ye lively portraiteers of Him whom ye are appointed to represent among men? Ye magistrates and rulers, are all the thoughts of your hearts, all your tempers and desires suitable to your high calling?"

Coming to the Fellows of the Colleges, among whom he included himself, he was even more direct. "What example is set the youth by us who enjoy the beneficence of our forefathers?" he asked. "Do you, brethren, abound in the fruits of the Spirit—in lowliness of mind, in self-denial and mortification, in patience, meekness, sobriety, temperance and an unwearied, restless endeavour to do good, in every kind unto all men? Is this the general character of Fellows of Colleges? I fear it is not. Rather have not pride and haughtiness of spirit, impatience, peevishness, sloth and in-dolence, gluttony, sensuality, even a proverbial uselessness, been objected to in us, perhaps not always by our enemies, nor wholly without ground?"

After dealing equally faithfully with the Fellows who were also ordained — the majority of the Fellows — and with the young students present, Wesley continued, "How few have any thought of God in the general tenor of your con' versation! Can you bear, and this now and then, in a church, any talk of the Holy Ghost? I ask, 'What religion are you of?' Even talk of Christianity ye cannot, will not bear. Oh my brethren! What a Christian city is this!"

It was at this point, says the Hebraist, Benjamin Kennicott, that the congregation felt that it had been given "a universal shock."

"What possibility is there," concluded Wesley, "that Christianity should again be the religion of this place? By whom should this Christianity be restored? By those of you who are in authority? Are you desirous that it should be restored? And do you not count your fortune, liberty, life dear unto you yourselves, so that you may be instrumental in restoring it? Perhaps some of you have made a few faint attempts, but with how small success? Shall Christianity then be restored by young, unknown, inconsiderable men? I know not whether ye yourselves would suffer it. Would not some of you cry out, 'Young man, in so doing thou reproachest us'? But there is no danger of your being put to the proof; so hath iniquity overspread us like a flood. Whom then shall God send? The famine, the pestilence of the sword, the last messengers of God to a guilty land?"

When Wesley walked out of the church into the sunlight, only three of his companions, his brother and two others, dared to speak to him.

Kennicott later summed up his impressions as follows: "I liked some of his freedom, such as calling the generality of young gownsmen 'a generation of triflers' and many other just invectives. But, considering how many shining lights are here that are the glory of the Christian cause, his sacred censure was much too flaming and strong. This, and the assertion that Oxford was not a Christian city and that this country not a Christian country, were the most offensive parts of his sermon. Had these things been omitted and his censures moderated, I think his discourse, as to style and delivery, would have been uncommonly pleasing to others as well as to myself." "I hear," Kennicott added, "the Heads of Houses intend to show their resentment." Blackstone added, "His notes were demanded by the Vice-Chancellor, but on matured deliberation it has been thought proper to punish him by a mortifying neglect."

Wesley took the whole thing as a matter of course. "I preached, I suppose the last time at St. Mary's," he wrote in his journal. "Be it so. I am now clear of the blood of these men. I have fully delivered my soul." He told how the Vice-Chancellor, the Provost of Oriel, had sent for the notes of his sermon. He added, "I sent them without delay, not without admiring the wise providence of God. Perhaps few men of note would have given a sermon of mine the reading if I had put it into their hands, but by this means it came to be read, probably more than once, by every man of eminence in the university."

In the early afternoon he left Oxford and never occupied the university pulpit again. From that time on, whenever his turn came around, the University paid another to preach in his stead.

"The message which it had now become Wesley's life work to deliver," writes M. R. Brailsford, "was peculiarly suited to the audiences which thronged to hear it. To these bru-talized, drink-sodden and neglected multitudes it brought the hope of new life. For their salvation in this world and the next it offered the strange panacea of faith in a young prophet, murdered judicially in a far foreign country two thousand years ago. And the miracle worked. For this Jesus was not only man, but God, and the Son of God: who, filled with pity for man's lost estate and for the still more desperate future which awaited them, had taken their fate upon His shoulders and died in their stead. . . . To men and women who were living without joy in the present or hope in the future this Gospel offered the love of an ever-present brother, the help and support of an all-powerful friend: and after this life a future of unimaginable riches and happiness. Faith alone was the key that could unlock this treasure-house. For those who have been nurtured in this creed from their mother's knee, it is hard to realize the overwhelming impact of its message upon the outcasts who in a Christian country had never heard the name of God except in blasphemy."

Above all, Wesley's message was practical. He was impatient of those who felt that if they mouthed cant phrases or repeated the correct theological formulae, they had done their duty. "I find more profit in sermons on either good tempers, or good works than in what are vulgarly called 'gospel sermons,'" he says. "Let a pert, self-sufficient animal that has neither sense nor grace bawl out something about Christ, or His blood, or justification by faith, and his hearers cry out 'What a fine gospel sermon!' We know no gospel without salvation from sin." "By salvation," he adds in *The Character of a Methodist*, "the Methodist means holiness of heart and life. It is nonsense for a woman to consider herself virtuous because she is not a prostitute or a man honest because he does not steal."

This concern with practical holiness made Wesley sparing in his reliance upon what he called "opinion." "There is no other religious society," he adds in 1788, "which requires nothing of men but the desire to save souls. The Methodists alone do not insist on your holding this opinion or that opinion: but they think and let think. Neither do they impose any particular mode of worship, but you may continue to worship in your former way, be it what it may." And again: "'Whosoever shall do the will of my Father which is in heaven, the same is my brother and sister and mother.'... For opinions and terms let us not destroy the work of God. Dost thou love and fear God? It is enough! I give you the right hand of fellowship."

Wesley showed this greatness of heart when, late in his life, his nephew Samuel, one of Charles' musical sons, became a Catholic at the age of eighteen. Charles raved about it because Samuel's conversion was due not to doctrine, but to his love of the Gregorian Service — within range of which Charles had brought his son by removing his family to London with the idea of forwarding his sons' musical education. John took it all with calm affection, and wrote: "I care not who is Head of the Church, provided you be a Christian. . . . My dear Sammy, your first point is to repent and believe the Gospel, . . . and then, if you have no better work, I will talk to you of transubstantiation and purgatory. . . ."

This is not to say that Wesley was indifferent to theology. He was a theologian before he was an evangelist, and, in a sense, his primary interest never ceased to be theological. It was through the stating of scriptural truth that he brought men to repentance and faith, and after they were converted he did not cease to instruct them in such truth to the end of their lives. He did not expound the whole body of Christian doctrine, not because he did not believe in it but because he felt that certain doctrines, through past neglect or through their extraordinary relevance, needed special emphasis. He took for granted that the doctrines of the creeds were true, and spent his time on those he regarded as immediately essential for man's salvation. So Rupert Davies speaks of

"Wesley's theology of the 'way to heaven' — to be believed and preached not as if it were the totality of Christian faith, but within the firm framework of the Creeds."

Just as Wesley emphasized those doctrines which showed men the way to heaven and which spread "scriptural holiness through the land," so he was only provoked to collision over doctrine when he saw God's grace denied or man's urge toward holiness discouraged. His difference with George Whitefield and others over predestination originated in the conviction that that doctrine represented God as "more false, more cruel and more unjust than the Devil, for it says that God has condemned millions of souls to continuing in sin which, for want of grace He gives them not, they are unable to avoid." This, he felt, must also discourage practical ho-liness. On the other hand, his own declaration that "free grace is free in all and free for all," while it ruled out all possibility of man earning anything through his own merit, yet left the door open to every man, and through hope stimulated all to holiness. Similarly, his difference with the Moravians, symbolized by his walking out of the Fetter Lane Society in 1740, was in protest against the extreme version of the Moravian doctrine of "stillness." He could not brook the idea that "you may as well go to Hell for praying as for thieving" — a statement made by those extremists who felt that to read the Bible or pray or go to communion until one had "perfect faith" was to seek salvation by works and therefore sinful.

Wesley's was essentially a social message. "Love of God and all mankind is the centre of religion," he wrote in 1743. "This love we believe to be the medicine of life, the never failing remedy for all the evils of a disordered world. Wherever it is, there are virtue and happiness hand in hand. There is humbleness of mind, gentleness, long suffering, the whole image of God and at the same time a peace that passeth all

understanding and joy unspeakable and full of glory." Christianity is, therefore, a social religion and "to turn it into a
solitary religion is to destroy it." "The gospel of Christ knows
no religion but social, no holiness but social holiness." As
Henry Carter wrote, "To Wesley a scheme to reconstruct
society which ignored the redemption of the individual was
unthinkable, but a doctrine to save sinning man, with no
aim to transform them into crusaders against social sin was
equally unthinkable."

SIX
It Takes More Than Preaching

Preaching was not Wesley's only — or even his main — concern during his fifty years of unrelenting service. "Mr. Wesley," wrote a contemporary when he was seventy-three, "is now an old man, and yet has such a variety and multiplicity of business as few men could manage, even in the prime of life. There are few weeks in which he does not travel two or three hundred miles; preach in public between twenty and thirty times, and often more; answer thirty or forty letters; speak with as many persons in private, concerning things of deep importance; and prepare, either in whole or in part, something for the Press." The same report could have been made of him at fifty — or at eighty.

In everything his first concern was with people. His practice was to speak to everybody he met about the "things of God." This was not always easy for him, but he regarded it as much a part of his commission as speaking to the thousands. On June 4, 1741, he described a two-day journey on a coach to Leicester. "For these two days," he wrote, "I have made an experiment which I had been so often and earnestly pressed to do — speaking to none concerning the things of God, unless my heart was free to it. But what was the event? Why? (1) That I spoke to none at all for four score miles together; no, not even to him that travelled with me in the chase, unless a few words at first setting out. (2) That I had no cross either to bear or to take up, and, in an hour or two fell fast asleep. (3) That I had much respect shown me wherever I came; everyone behaving to me as to a civil good natured gentleman. Oh, how pleasing is all this to flesh and blood! Need ye 'compass sea and land' to make proselytes to this?"

Wesley's concern was for the individual, regardless of class. "The dog enchants us with his conversation," complained Dr. Johnson, "and then breaks off to visit some old woman." Wesley realized that the whole health of his society depended on this personal work. "I am determined at least once in every three months to talk to every member myself and to enquire at their own mouths whether they grow in grace," he said once. "At these seasons I likewise enquire whether there is any misunderstanding or difference between them." Of another three days which he spent "speaking severally" to members of the Bristol Society, he writes, "As many of them increase in wealth and worldly goods, the great danger I apprehend is their relapsing into the spirit of the world; and then their religion is but a dream."

In all his contacts he was faithful to the resolve he made in Oxford in 1731 — that he would never "give anyone up till he disclaims my help *totidem verbis* or I have tried him for ten years." He also approached all individuals with great faith in their possibilities. In the days when many of his members claimed to have been spiritually "perfected" he listened to them with infinite patience and faith and believed that it could happen to them, although he never claimed that he had been "perfected" himself. Charles often scolded him for a too-easy belief in others, and sometimes Charles proved right. But it is fair to say that it was John's generous spirit, rather than Charles' sometimes censorious one, which created and sustained the awakening — and which inspired the field preachers to face persecution and death to spread their faith.

It was John's concern for individuals which made him found societies wherever he went. "Preaching like an apostle, without joining together those that are awakened, and training them in the way of God, is only begetting children for the murderer," he noted. "How much preaching has there been for these twenty years in Pembrokeshire! But no regular societies, no discipline, order or connection; and the consequence is that nine in ten of the once awakened are now faster asleep than ever."

The truth of this was borne out in America. There, tens of thousands of people had been converted by Whitefield's preaching. But Whitefield felt he had not the aptitude for founding and nurturing societies, so most of them faded away. Whitefield himself once described it as "weaving a rope of sand." Wesley, on the other hand, grasped what was involved in winning, confirming, and setting men to work so that the nation would be "reformed," and he faced the labor of doing the work necessary.

Indeed, he sensed this situation from the first. The very day after he first preached in the open air in Bristol, he formed two societies for those whom Whitefield and he were changing. A month later, he had acquired a piece of ground for the first preaching house there. Meanwhile, he had visited Bath — where he had his victorious encounter with Beau Nash — and had founded societies there. In London, during that winter of 1739, some people affected by his and Whitefield's preaching came to Wesley and asked to meet with him each Thursday evening. When they reached one hundred in number, he took down their names and formed a society. As winter came on — it was the bitterest in living memory — and he found himself still drawing crowds of eight thousand a night, he looked around for a suitable meeting place. He was directed to "a vast, uncouth heap of ruins," the Foundry at Moorfields, from which the casting of the royal cannon had been removed, after an explosion, to Woolwich. Here he built his London headquarters — not for the sake of having headquarters, but because people needed it.

Class meetings evolved to meet a similar need. It all started in Bristol on February 15, 1744, during a discussion about how to clear the debt on the new preaching house. A certain Captain Foy, a seafaring man, suggested that every member of the Society should contribute a penny a week. When it was objected that many were too poor for that, Foy replied: "Then put ten or twelve of them to me. I will visit them each week. Let each of them give what they can, and I will supply what is wanting." So it was decided, and the Bristol society was divided into little companies or classes of about twelve each.

The plan succeeded, and Wesley, who knew the importance of money but was never bounded by it, swiftly saw the spiritual possibilities. "This is the very thing," he declared, "the very thing we have wanted for so long." He saw in it the vehicle for personal help and supervision throughout his societies, which were by now far too large and numerous for his unaided personal supervision. So first the London Society of over two thousand and then those throughout the country were divided into classes on the Bristol model, each with its appointed leader. Before long it was found difficult to maintain visiting — masters and mistresses did not always like their servants receiving such — and so the class members began to meet together somewhere for an hour once or twice a week.

The idea was that the weak were encouraged and assisted by the stronger. The atmosphere aimed at was one of absolute honesty and complete trust — in God and in each other.

Often the sexes were conveniently divided, and the most pressing and intimate problems of life could be discussed and "raised aloft" in the certain hope of forgiveness and victory. All members were pledged to secrecy regarding any personal confessions. Here tens of thousands of ordinary men and women learned to take the further steps of change and thousands of leaders learned to lead. Class leaders were encouraged to make some report to Wesley himself every three months, and it was through these ten thousand and more lay pastors that Wesley kept such close touch with his people. It was to visit these leaders, as well as to preach to the populace at large, that he undertook his endless journeying.

"In the preaching meetings," writes Bready, "people caught their vision and turned toward their goal. In the class meetings they found their spiritual school where, under trusted leaders, they grouped together in mutual aid to work out their salvation and to discuss reverently and prayerfully their attitude to social, ethical, and religious problems of their daily life." "The class leaders," he adds, "were chiefly men and women at whom the smart, fashionable world long laughed; but even blatant cynicism came in time to be hushed before their sincerity and their integrity. Their wisdom was penetrating, for it came of a regenerated heart and expressed itself in loving fellowship with all, who 'followed after what they knew they had not yet attained.'"

The organizational feat was considerable. Almost every movement since that day—from the Abolitionists, through the Chartists to the Trade Unions and the Communist Party—have adopted his cellular method. But the motive was, for Wesley, not power, but the care of people.

* * *

Wesley's greatest care was in choosing and training his lay preachers and class leaders. Before his death there were seven hundred full-time lay preachers in England alone and another three hundred and fifty in America. These were men of heroic stature. For them "no road was too boggy, no weather too inclement, no ford too swollen, no community too degraded, no mob too violent, no privation too severe." The Welshman, Olivers, traveled not less than a hundred thousand miles on one horse. Another, John Pritchard, his horse worn out, journeyed twelve hundred miles on foot in a single winter. Mitchell was thrown into a pond at night, and repeatedly hurled back when he tried to get out. Nelson was beaten unconscious and left for dead by some "Yorkshire gentlemen." John Downe's widow was left with only six-pence in the world, while John Jane died worth one and fourpence—"enough," says Wesley, "for an unmarried preacher of the Gospel to leave to his executors." "For what pay would you procure men to do this service, to be always ready to go to prison or to death?" asked Wesley. "They carried their lives in their hands," he said on another occasion. "Both the great vulgar and the small looked on them as mad dogs, and treated them as such, sometimes saying in terms: will nobody knock that mad dog on the head?"

They had to face the harder trial of their wives and children being persecuted. "When I got home," wrote John Nelson once, "I found my wife much better though never likely to recover her former strength owing to the persecution she met with at Wakefield when Mr. Larwood was mobbed there. After they had abused him, she, with some women, set out for Birstall. A mob followed them into the field. When they overtook them she turned about and spake to them; upon which all the men returned without touching them; but the women followed them till they came to a gate, where they stopped them; they damned her saying: 'You are Nelson's wife, and here you shall die.' They saw she was big with child, yet beat her on the body so cruelly that they killed the child in her womb; and she went home and miscarried directly. This treatment she had reason to remember to her life's end; but God more than made it up to her by filling her with peace and love."

There was hardly among them a man of breeding or learning. Nelson was a stonemason, Pawson the son of a small farmer, Olivers and Mather the sons of tradesmen. Laurence Sterne called these men "illiterate mechanics, more fitted to make a pulpit than to get into one." But Wesley was nearer the point when at the age of sixty-nine he wrote to Dublin, "By this time I should be some judge of men; and if I am, all England and Ireland cannot afford such a body of men, number for number, for sense and true experience both of men and things, as the body of Methodist preachers." "In the one thing they profess to know," he added once, "they are not ignorant men. I trust there is not one of them who is not able to go through such an examination in substantial, practical, experimental divinity as few of our graduates for Holy Orders even in the university (I speak it in sorrow and shame and tender love) are able to do."

The preachers owed this, in large measure, to Wesley's training of them. He was accustomed to examine each candidate on three points: Has he grace? Has he gifts? Has he fruit? On being offered the help of a clergyman in 1742 — when clergymen in his work were as rare as gold — Wesley writes, "I cannot suddenly answer in this matter; I must first know what spirit he is of; for none can labour with us unless he 'count all things dung and dross, that he may win Christ.'" For him neither scholarship nor genius was a substitute for purity and piety.

At the Leeds Conference of 1753, the famous *Rules for a Helper* were drawn up. The essential points of the *Rules* were:

Be diligent. Never be unemployed for a moment. . . .

Converse sparingly with women; particularly with young women in private.

Take no step towards marriage without acquainting us with your design.

Believe evil of no one. . . .

Speak evil of no one. . . .

Do not affect the gentleman. You have no more to do with this character than with that of a dancing master. A Preacher of the Gospel is the servant of all.

Be ashamed of nothing but sin: not of fetching wood (if time permit), or drawing water: not of cleaning your own shoes, or your neighbours'.

Be punctual. Do everything exactly at the time. And, in general, do not mend our rules, but keep them. . . .

You have nothing to do but to save souls. Therefore spend and be spent in the work. . . .

Observe. It is not your business to preach so many times . . . but to save as many souls as you can. . . . Therefore you will need all the sense you have, and to have your wits about you.

The preachers were divided by Wesley into twelve circuits, and the leading preacher in each was called the "assistant." Wesley set for them a strict standard of working, one which he observed himself.

Thus at the 1745 Conference it was decided that preachers, besides preaching every morning and every night, must spend from six to twelve every day in reading, writing, and prayer; from twelve to five in visiting; and from five to six in private communion with God.

We see Wesley's thought clearly in his address at the Conference of 1766 concerning "a thorough reform of the preachers." "The world says, 'Methodists are no better than other people,'" he began. "This is not true. Yet it is nearer the truth than we are willing to imagine. Personal religion is amazingly superficial amongst us. How little faith there is amongst us, how little communion with God! How much love of the world! Desire of pleasure, of ease, of praise, of getting money, how little brotherly love, what continual judging one of another, what gossiping, evil speaking, tale bearing, what want of moral honesty! . . . And the Methodists in general will be little better, till we take quite another course with them." He goes on to say that the preachers must visit from house to house, that they must know every person in the house and have personal dealing in detail with them. "Let us set upon this in good earnest," he continues, "and we shall soon find why the people are not better, namely, because we are not more *knowing* and more *holy*."

"Why are we not more knowing?" he continues. "Because we are idle. We forget the very first rule, 'be diligent, never be unemployed a moment, never be triflingly employed, never wile away time, never spend any more time at any place than is strictly necessary.' I fear there is altogether a fault in this matter and that few of us are clear. Which of us spends as many hours a day in God's work, as you did formerly in man's work? We must, absolutely must cure this evil, or give up the whole work. But how?

"Spend all the morning, or at least five hours in twenty-four in reading the most useful books and that regularly and constantly. 'But I read only the Bible.' Then you ought to teach others to read only the Bible and by parity of reason to hear only the Bible. But if so, you need preach no more. If you need no book but the Bible, you are got above St. Paul, he wanted others too. 'But I have no taste for reading.' Contract a taste for it by use or return to your trade. 'But different men have different tastes.' Therefore some may read less than others; but none should read less than this. 'But I have no books.' I will give each of you as fast as you can read them books to the value of £5; and I desire the assistant to take care that all large societies provide the Christian Library for the use of preachers."

From "knowing" he passed to "holiness." "Why are we not more holy?" he asked. "Answer — to touch upon only two or three instances. Do you rise at four? Or even at five, when you do not preach? Do you fast once a week? Once a month? Do you know the obligation or benefit of it? Do you recommend the five o'clock hour for private prayer? Do you observe it? Do you not find that any time is no time?"

So he proceeds with question after practical question in his passion to make every preacher a prophet. He succeeded because he practiced what he preached.

He himself spent much time writing. In forty years, during which he traveled twenty-five miles most days, he wrote 233 books. No wonder a contemporary remarked that those who knew his writings wondered that he had the time to travel, while those who knew his travels wondered how he had any time to write. Sometimes he had to take up the cudgels in controversy, but he did not choose it. "Heavy work," he wrote after replying to Bishop Lavington of Exeter, "such as I should never choose; but sometimes it must be done." His motive was quite different. "Two and forty years ago," he wrote in 1780, "having a desire to furnish other people with cheaper, shorter and plainer books than anything I had seen, I wrote many small tracts, generally a penny a piece, and afterwards several larger." His larger projects included his Christian Library where, in some eighty volumes, he tried to "condense all that is most valuable in the English tongue." These were the books that were studied by every lay preacher and all the class leaders. They were one of the greatest educative forces of the age. Among them was a *Complete English Dictionary*, printed in 1753, with the curious subtitle "Explaining most of the Hard Words which are found in the Best English Writers. By a Lover of Good English and Common Sense. N.B. — the Author assures you he thinks this the best English Dictionary in the world." In his preface to the Dictionary, Wesley's sly humor peeps out:

"I have often observed the only way, according to modern taste, for any Author to procure commendation of his Book is vehemently to praise it himself. For want of this deference to the Publick, several excellent Tracts lately printed . . . are utterly unknown or forgotten. Whereas, if a writer of tolerable Sense will but bestow a few violent Encomiums on his own Work . . . it will pass through six editions in a trice — the World being too complaisant to give the Gentle-man the lie, and taking it for granted he understands his own performance best. . . . Many are the Mistakes in all the other English Dictionaries which I have yet seen. Whereas I can truly say I know of none in this — and I conceive the Reader will believe me: for if I had, I should not have left them there."

John himself seldom wrote original hymns. But his trans-lations of various German hymns, often artistically finer than the originals, showed his true powers, and one understands Dr. Leger's high opinion of the Wesleys' influence in preparing the way for the Romantic movement. The hymn book which John compiled in Georgia was the first of its kind, and his 1780 collection of Methodist hymns was used without al-teration for a hundred years.

Monsignor Knox is critical of Wesley's literary standards. He wrote nothing, says Knox, to compare with Butler, he is little read today, he is a popularizer, his mind is not pro-found. And again: "'No man,' he tells us, 'should be above writing correctly,' and the adverb is revealing. He was too much a child of his age to forsake the grand manner; too much a child of light to achieve the grand manner really well."

Mgr. Knox explains this phenomenon when he calls Wesley "a utilitarian concentrated," in his writing as in everything else, "on the one thing needful"; yet for a moment one feels that the don in Knox has taken over from the Christian. Wesley did not want to charm, but to convert, not to win the applause of Oxford, but to educate the laboring men, the men of Tolpuddle, for example, who were to become the backbone of the future age. Nor must it be forgotten that it was one of Wesley's sermons which Manning was clutching in his hands that day in the Charing Cross Road when he first told his friend that he had been brought to God. Wesley, too, could have inhabited that world of Oxford had he wished. He preferred to roam the world, preach the sermons and write the books necessary for the greatest re-awakening of British history—a reawakening which was in the end to do almost as much, through Manning and New-man, for Knox's Church as for the Church of Knox's father.

Knox quotes a saying that it is difficult to say whether Wesley's enormous circulation was a tribute to his literary powers or to his power of imposing his will. There is also the possibility that Wesley may have produced what, at that moment, plain men wanted to read. All the same, Wesley had great faith in the power of books, and expected his itinerants to promote their sale. "I sometimes wonder that all our preachers are not convinced of this: that it is of unspeakable use to spread our practical tracts in every so-ciety," he wrote to Thomas Rankin. "Billy Pennington, in one year, sold more of these in Cornwall than had been sold for seven years before. So may you if you take the same methods. Carry one sort of book with you the first time you go round the round; another sort the second time; and so on. Preach on the subject at each place; after preaching encourage the congregation to buy and read the tract. Peace be with your spirit!"

To another of his preachers he wrote of a recent tract: "Enforce it both in public and private conversation. Spare no pains. Exert yourself. See what you can do. Give this proof of your love for the truth for the people and for your affectionate friend and brother, John Wesley."

It has often been said that the awakening succeeded be-cause John Wesley, unlike Charles and Whitefield, had a genius for government and organization. It would be truer to say that he had that supreme love of people, which saw that winning men and changing society meant more than preaching or hymn-writing, or any other one activity. It meant the rounded work which supplied thousands of people with the change and training, the fellowship and action which could establish them and make them changers of their nation.

Well past his eightieth year Wesley continued these labors. Tyerman writes, "Here we have — not a man of Herculean frame, big, brawny and heavy, fed on the daintiest diet and stimulated with costliest wine — but a man small in stature, his weight eight stone and ten pounds, his age eighty, without indulgences, feeding for eight months in the year chiefly at the tables of the poor, sleeping on all sorts of beds and in all sorts of rooms, without a wife, without a child, really without a home; and yet a man always cheerful, always happy, always hard at work, flying with all the sprightliness of youth throughout the three kingdoms; preaching twice every day indoors and out-of-doors, in churches, chapels, cottages and sheds and everywhere superintending the com-plex and varying interests of the numerous societies which had sprung into being through the labours of himself and his helpers. The man was a marvel, such as the world only sees now and then. Once show him the path of duty and with a dauntless step he trod it. Nothing frightened him; nothing could lure him from the post assigned him by Providence. However arduous the work and however great the privations and the dangers, he went trusting in his Master's power for defence and help. 'My brother, Charles,' he once remarked, 'amid the difficulties of our early ministry used to say, "If the Lord would give me wings I would fly." I used to reply, 'If the Lord bade me fly, I would trust Him for the wings.'"

SEVEN
Men on Trial

During the first three decades of the awakening, the violent interference of the mobs was more or less continuous. Times out of number, the meetings of Wesley and his friends were attacked by gangs armed with clubs, whips, bricks, stink bombs, wildfire, or rotten eggs. Sometimes bulls were driven through the audience or horsemen overrode them. Sometimes the interrupters merely tried to drown the preacher's voice with bells, drums, tin cans, or horns.

In Colne, Lancashire, in 1748, Wesley was struck in the face and then felled to the ground "by ruffians raging like lions," while Grimshaw was loaded "with mire and dirt of every kind" and Mackford dragged by his hair through the mud. Meanwhile the whole congregation, women and men, old and young, were pelted with stones. Many, too, were beaten with clubs, some sustaining permanent injury. "All this time," Wesley records, the Rev. George White, self-styled "Commander-in-Chief" of the mob, sat nearby "well-pleased," "talking of justice and law" and "not attempting in the least to hinder them." White, who had posted a proclamation calling up the mob "for the defence of the Church of England and the Support of the Manufactory in

77

and about Colne" and promising every man alcoholic encouragement before going into battle, subsequently drank
himself to death.

Another famous riot was at Wednesbury. Here the mob,
"hired by their betters" and "bound by an oath" to "plunder
all the Methodists in Wednesbury" began on Shrove Tuesday, 1744, by breaking all the windows of Methodist homes.
Then "all the tables, chairs, chest of drawers, with whatever
was not easily removeable they dashed to pieces," while
unbreakables, such as feather beds, "they cut in pieces and
strewed about the room." Finding the wife of William Sitch
"lying in," they pulled her bed away from her and cut that
to pieces, too. All clothes and valuables they carried away.
Then, "some of the gentlemen who had set the mob to work
or had threatened to turn away collier or miner out of their
service if he did not come and do his part drew up a paper
for those of the Society to sign importing that they would
never invite or receive any Methodist preacher again." The
Methodists refused to sign it and said, "We have already
lost all our goods; and nothing more can follow, but the loss
of our lives which we will lose too rather than wrong our
consciences." So the orgy continued, until the houses of
some hundreds of Wesley's disciples in and around Wednesbury resembled a "devastated area." Most of the Methodists were stripped of all they had in the world. As a final
irony the London *Evening Post* of February 18, 1744, reported that there had been "an insurrection of the people
called Methodists in Wednesbury who, upon some pretended
insults from the Church Party, had assembled themselves
in a riotous manner and having committed several outrages
proceeded at last to burn the houses of their adversaries."
Actually the Methodists had made no resistance as they
realized that this was the only way they could protect their
women-folk.

Generally, there were "gentlemen" or clergy behind these riots. Wesley describes many such incidents, often with an eye for humor. At North Taunton the clergyman "with two or three by the courtesy of England called gentlemen" began an uproar, Wesley wrote in 1765. "They had brought a huntsman with his hounds; but the dogs were wiser than the men, for they would not bring them to make any noise at all. One of the gentlemen supplied their place. He assured us he was such, though none would have suspected it; for his language was as base, foul, and porterly as was ever heard at Billingsgate." On September 19, 1769, Wesley noted, "The beasts were tolerably quiet until I had nearly finished my sermon. They then lifted up their voice, especially one, called a gentleman, who had filled his pockets with rotten eggs: but a young man coming unawares, kept his hand on each side, and mashed them all at once. In an instance he was perfume all over; though it was not so sweet as balsam."

Magistrates, in general, afforded no protection. Some even advised mobs to "do what you will" with the Methodists, "so you break no bones." Others issued general warrants for the arrest of itinerant preachers. While more than once, fuming gentlemen contracted with mobs to "drive all that are called Methodists" out of the district. Dr. Borlase, the Cornish magistrate, clergyman, and scholar, when asked by James Dale for justice against an anti-Methodist mob which had smashed his house and plundered his goods, yelled out: "Thou conceited fellow. What! Art thou turned religious? They may burn thy house if they will; it is no concern of mine." "I asked a little gentleman of St. Just," writes Wesley, "what objection there was to Edward Greenfield. He said, 'Why, the man is well enough in other things; but his impudence the gentleman cannot bear. Why, sir, he says he knows his sins are forgiven!'"

Wesley came through it all with superb courage. He never

lost his temper and was always ready to take a blow if that would ease his assailants' hysteria. When struck by a stone, he would quietly wipe away the blood and go on speaking. He always looked a mob in the face, and it was his custom — and Charles' too — to hurry to the scene of hottest persecution. "If he had been a soldier on active service," says Vulliamy, "people would have said that his life was charmed. Stones, aimed at him, missed their mark or hit the enemy instead. Cudgels were thrust aside, or knocked out of murderous hands, by some invisible force. It was not courage alone that saved Wesley. He was preserved by tranquil dignity, by cool, steady and courteous behavior, by the entire absence of malice and anger, but above all by those peculiar graces and powers which accompany a man of God."

More important, his serenity first broke, then won, the heart of many a mob leader. In Walsall, in 1743, when he was only spared death because the mob leaders could not decide how to kill him, a man raised his arm to brain him, then gently laid his hand on Wesley's head saying: "What soft hair he has!" Others, who thrust fiercely toward him, found themselves powerless in his immediate presence. The mob thrust him down a hill, but as Charles relates: "His feet never once slipped: for in their hands the angels bore him up. . . . The spirit of glory rested on him. As many as he spoke to, or but laid a hand on him, he turned into friends." At the most critical moment, when all seemed lost, a hulking fellow, one of the leaders, stepped up to him and said: "Sir, I will spend my life for you: follow me, and not one soul here shall touch a hair of your head." At this the leaders of the gang turned into an escort, and saw him to safety.

His own account of a visit to Falmouth, in July 1745, carries the atmosphere of those years:

"I rode to Falmouth. About three in the afternoon I went to see a gentlewoman who had long been indisposed. Almost as soon as I sat down, the house was beset on all sides by an innumerable multitude of people. A louder or more confused noise could hardly be at the taking of a city by storm. At first Mrs. B. and her daughter endeavoured to quiet them. But it was labour lost. They might as well have attempted to still the raging of the sea. . . . The rabble roared with all their throats: 'Bring out the Canorum! Where is the Canorum?' [A meaningless word which the Cornish generally use instead of Methodist.]

"No answer being given, they quickly forced open the outer door, and filled the passage. Only a wainscot partition was between us, which was not likely to stand long. I immediately took down a large looking-glass which hung against it, supposing the whole side would fall in at once. When they began their work, with abundance of bitter imprecations, poor Kitty [the maid] was utterly astonished, and cried out: 'O sir, what must we do?' I said: 'We must pray.' Indeed at that time, to all appearance, our lives were not worth an hour's purchase. . . . Among those without were the crews of some privateers, which were lately come into harbour. Some of these, being angry at the slowness of the rest, thrust them away, and coming up all together, set their shoulders to the inner door, and cried out: 'Avast, lads, avast!' Away went all the hinges at once, and the door fell back into the room.

"I stepped forward at once into the midst of them, and said: 'Here I am. Which of you has anything to say to me? To which of you have I done any wrong? To you? Or you? Or you?' I continued speaking till I came, bareheaded as I was (for I purposely left my hat that they might all see my face), into the middle of the street, and then raising my voice, said: 'Neighbours, countrymen! Do you desire to hear me speak?' They cried vehemently: 'Yes, yes! He shall speak! He shall! Nobody shall hinder him!' But having nothing to stand on, and no advantage of ground, I could be heard by few only. However, I spoke without intermission, and, as far as the sound reached, the people were still; till one or two of their captains turned about and swore, not a man would touch him."

But Wesley's persistent courage did more than win men — it won towns and communities. Take, for example, St. Ives in Cornwall. In 1743, a roaring gang broke into the room there when he was speaking. Wesley tried to persuade his people to stand still. "But the zeal of some and the fear of others had no ears," he writes. "So that, finding the uproar increase, I went into the midst and brought the head of the mob to the desk. I received but one blow on the side of the head; after which we reasoned the case, till he grew milder and milder, and at length undertook to quiet his companions."

In 1745, there was a small disturbance in the street at St. Ives. "We expected a visit in the evening from some of the devil's drunken champions who swarm here on a holyday, so called; but none appeared," said Wesley. A year later, in 1746, Wesley noted that "many were there who had been vehement opposers; but from this time they opposed no more." In 1753 he examined the society in St. Ives. "I found an accursed thing among them: well-nigh one and all bought or sold uncustomed goods. I told them plain, either they must put this abomination away, or they would see my face no more." Next day, he notes: "They severally promised so to do." In 1760 he preached to "well-nigh the whole town, low and high, rich and poor," in the middle of a great storm — and again in 1789 "well-nigh the whole town attended and with all possible seriousness. Surely forty years' labour has not been in vain here." So it was in Colne, Walsall, Wednesbury, and many other communities.

But physical persecution was only the most spectacular of the opposition to Wesley and his companions. The spoken,

printed, and whispered word was the background to vio-
lence, for then, as now, it created the climate of opinion.
Already by 1740 over a hundred pamphlets had been issued
against the Wesleys and Whitefield. Pulpits were not only
closed to them, but were used to vilify them. "Every
Sunday," remarks Charles Wesley, "damnation is pronounced
against us, for we are Papists, Jesuits, seducers and bringers-
in of the Pretender."

The slanders were many and varied, not to say contra-
dictory. In England they were called Popish and pro-French;
in Ireland anti-Pope and pro-English. One clergyman accused
them of being adulterers and maintaining an immoral house
at the Foundry, while a Bishop said they put the claims of
religion too high and so discouraged people from seeking it.
Some said they encouraged education in the poor; others
that they ignored the intellect; some that they were self-
willed dictators; others that they were cowardly in expecting
God to make up their minds for them. Any stick was good
enough with which to beat the dog. And generally the stick
was not the point. The point was the urge, the itch, the
sting which made them want to use the stick at all.

In some cases the motive was obvious. The comment in
the *Gentleman's Magazine* upon Whitefield's preaching to
the miners of Kingswood is such a case: "The industry of
the inferior People in a Society," the writer said, "is the great
Source of its Prosperity. But if one Man like the Rev. Mr.
Whitefield, should have the Power, by his Preaching to
detain five or six thousands of the Vulgar from their daily
Labour, what a loss, in a little Time, may this bring to the
Publick! For my part, I shall expect to hear of a prodigious
Rise in the Price of Coals about the City of Bristol, if this
Gentleman proceeds, as he has begun, with his charitable
Lectures to the Colliers of Kingswood."

The motivations of the Duchess of Buckingham are also

clear. This illegitimate daughter of James II wrote to Lady Huntingdon: "I thank Your Ladyship for the information concerning the Methodist preachers: their doctrines are most repulsive, strongly tinctured with Impertinence and Disrespect towards their Superiors, in perpetually endeavouring to level all Ranks, and do away with all Distinctions. It is monstrous to be told that you have a heart as *sinful* as the Common Wretches that crawl on the Earth. This is highly offensive and insulting; and I can not but wonder that Your Ladyship should relish any Sentiment so much at variance with High Rank and Good Breeding."

Less immediately transparent was the motive of the popular London preacher, Dr. Dodd, who officiated at the Chapel in Palace Street, Westminster. A foppish man, sometimes called "the macaroni parson," he was nevertheless a royal chaplain and honorary canon of Brecon and his word swayed many when, from pulpit and in pamphlet, he attacked Wesley and his friends for thinking themselves perfect. True, his reputation went under a temporary cloud when, in 1774, it was discovered that he had tried to bribe the Lord Chancellor's wife to the tune of 3,000 pounds to get him the rectorship of St. George's, Hanover Square, but by 1777 he was drawing large and fashionable crowds to hear him once more. In that year, however, he was discovered to have forged a bill of 4,200 pounds on the name of his former pupil, Lord Chesterfield, and was condemned to death by hanging. Dodd must have known where the truth lay, for it was to the Wesleys that he turned in his hour of need. He implored John to visit him in prison, and John, who went unwillingly, believing that Dodd only wanted him to use his influence on his behalf, found that Dodd "entirely and calmly gave himself up to the will of God."

Perhaps, too, Horace Walpole's antagonism was not unconnected with his spiteful nature — nor with the fact that during his lifetime he received some 200,000 pounds from the government for doing little except being the son of Sir Robert Walpole.

Of course, there were occasions when people were put off by something the Wesleys had done, or were thought to have done. Bishop Lavington's enmity began when a malicious printer issued a pamphlet purporting to be an extract from his 1748 Episcopal Charge, but which was in fact quite fictitious and which exposed him to the stigma of being regarded a Methodist. The Bishop suspected the Wesleys of the fraud and was with difficulty shown that they had no part in the deception. Nevertheless, from that time he became a "fervent hater of the Methodists" — and his scurrilous diatribes in the next fourteen years were filled with profanity and malice. The Bishop died in 1762, and it is pleasant to read in Wesley's journal that Wesley visited Exeter Cathedral fifteen days before the Bishop's death where he "was well pleased to partake of the Lord's Supper with my old opponent."

But whether the antagonism was gratuitous, or had some initial excuse as in the case of Bishop Lavington, the fact remains that Wesley was, on the whole, persecuted not for his mistakes but for his glories, not for being wrong but for being right. Through him and his friends the Holy Spirit was manifestly at work in Britain on a larger scale than for many generations, if not centuries. It was the Spirit which he served which people found uncomfortable. It pierced them at many places as it challenged the greed, lust, or vested interest of even the most respectable.

Such is the mark of the Spirit. It acts as a kind of geiger counter for the motives of men and nations. It was Simeon, looking upon the baby Jesus, who said: "This child is destined to be a sign which men reject. . . . Many in Israel will stand or fall because of him, and *thus the secret thoughts of many will be laid bare.*" Men reveal themselves by their reaction. With some, like Dodd, the reason for rejection becomes plain, while with others it is never clear to the public in their lifetime. But now, after two hundred years, it is easy to see that it was not Wesley, but eighteenth-century England, that was on trial.

EIGHT
The Church Recumbent

No institution was on trial more than the Church of England. The eighteenth-century church was renowned for scholarship, culture, and doctrinal tolerance, but one which — at a time when it had the official monopoly of caring for the spiritual needs of the whole people — left the entire industrial working class untouched, and distrusted as "enthusiasm" any attempt to reach them. There were many fine Christians in the church, especially in the country parishes and "little" bishoprics; and because of them, as Overton says, "sufficient salt was left to preserve the mass from becoming utterly corrupt." But the admired churchmen of the age were the scholar-statesman Bishop Gibson of London or the sheerly political Bishop Hoadly, who never once, in six years, found time to visit his diocese of Bangor.

For the Church of England was primarily a department of state responsible for ecclesiastical affairs — and the maintenance of the status quo. At a time when government majorities in the House of Lords were insured by the adroit use of patronage, bishops were chosen for political, not spiritual reasons. Their twenty-six votes in an average attendance of one hundred and twenty were an important matter, and they were expected to vote with the government of the day. This entailed their spending eight months in London each year, and in their dioceses, too, they were expected to be a center of loyalty and government propaganda.

This situation was, in part, a legacy of the Civil War, when doctrinal quarrels were a main reason for Englishmen killing each other. In 1662, two thousand Puritan-leaning clergy — including both of Wesley's grandparents — had been removed from their livings, while in 1689 those among the bishops and clergy who still considered James to be lawful king were similarly deprived. This weeding out of the strong spirits of left and right had impoverished the church. That it was accepted shows the horror of the nation at the strife which "enthusiasm" in religion was seen to have caused in the previous century.

The new age was tolerant — and sceptical. "Scepticism, widely diffused through the upper classes, was of that in-dolent variety, implying a perfect willingness that the churches should survive, though the faith should perish," writes Sir Leslie Stephen. "The notion that it was necessary to preserve the Establishment in order to secure the obedience of the vulgar," adds Temperley, "was accepted by Walpole, who confessed himself a sceptic in private, but publicly proclaimed his adherence to the Church, and by Bolingbroke who outdid him alike in the secret fervour of his free-thinking and the open passion of his orthodoxy. . . . Nothing could be worse for a religion or a Church than a public adherence to its forms and a private ridiculing of its substance by a large proportion of the governing class."

Standards of style were exacting, but morals were lax. The leaders of the church, however, seem to have kept free from sexual license. "For the most part," writes J. H. Plumb, "they [the clergy] were steady commonplace men, inclined to toryism, strongly distrustful of all change and innovation, unmoved by the deeper problems of religious faith, who nevertheless tended their flocks with care and charity. Often they acted as physicians and lawyer as well as parson. . . . About most of their lives there was a steady, self-indulgent benevolence which comes to men locked in a narrow world of easy circumstances. But for the ambitious clergyman there was but one way to advancement: a well-placed patron, and unwavering devotion to politics."

Dodsley, writing in the year of Wesley's conversion, touched on the effects of patronage in *The Art of Preaching*:

> When dukes or noble lords a chaplain hire
> They first of his capacities enquire.
> If stoutly qualified to drink and smoke,
> If not too nice to bear an impious joke,
> If tame enough to be the common jest,
> This is the chaplain to his lordship's taste.

And the chaplaincy was the road to preferment. For, as Dr. Johnson roundly stated on Good Friday 1775, "No man can now be made a bishop for his learning and piety; his only chance of promotion is his being connected with someone who has a parliamentary interest." Certainly, you had to conform to reach one of the plum dioceses. Thus, in 1782, Dr. Richard Watson was elevated to the see of Llandaff, worth perhaps 500 pounds a year, because he had written a pamphlet about America which happened, almost by accident, to support Lord Shelburne's policy. But he stuck in Llandaff for thirty-three years because "I could not bring myself to vote as a minister bade me on all occasions; and I perceived that . . . nothing less . . . would secure his attention." Hoadly, on the other hand, never took an independent step and so, between 1721 and 1734, progressed from Bangor to Hereford to Salisbury, and finally on to the high prize of Winchester, worth 5,000 pounds a year.

Not that Bishop Watson had much to complain about, though complain he did. "The provision of £2,000 a-year which I possess from the church," he wrote, "arises from the tithes of two churches in Shropshire, two in Leicester-shire, two in my diocese, three in Huntingdonshire, on all of which I have resident curates; of five more appropriations to the bishopric, and two more in the Isle of Ely as appro-priations to the archdeaconry of Ely." As there was no official residence in Llandaff, he settled in comfortable quarters "in the beautiful districts on the banks of Winandermere" and made but rare visits to his diocese.

The Archbishops of Canterbury in this century are an interesting study. John Potter (1737–47), the Primate at the time of Wesley's conversion, was, A. W. Rowden says, "stilted and starchy"[1] and, true to the current fashion of the ruling class into which he (a draper's son) had been lifted, left behind him 90,000 pounds which he had "saved out of the church." Potter's successor, Thomas Herring (1747–57) was "less worthy than he." Matthew Hutton (1757–58), "died in time for his character; for he was grown cov-etous and imperious to excess. He left £50,000 which he had saved out of the church in twelve years, and not one penny to good use or public charity."[2] Thomas Secker (1758–68) was the best of the bunch, a kindly hard-working Primate but "too much victimized by the frigid rationalism domi-nating superior society" to offer real direction to the church. He was succeeded by Frederick Cornwallis (1768–83) who according to Perry's *History of the Church of England*, "appears to have had no churchman-like scruples and was simply of the character of a great nobleman about court." John Moore (1783–1805) was the most nepotic Primate of the age. He secured well-feathered nests for five sons, three as Joint-Registrars of the Prerogative Court of Canterbury and the other two as Joint-Registrars of the Vicar-General's Office.[3] One son received "not less than £12,000" annually for fifty years. By contrast, missionaries sent out to the Indians in North America in the eighteenth century earned between ten and thirty pounds a year, and over four thousand English clergy received between fifty and 150 pounds annually. "It is extremely difficult," explains Overton, "for any man to rise above the spirit of his age. He who can do so is a spiritual hero. . . . It surely does not follow that because a man cannot be a hero he must therefore be a bad man." True. But it is fair to add that followers of Christ who failed so conspicuously to rise above their age as did the Primates of the century could hardly hope to understand a man like Wesley.

Nor is it surprising that a church led by such men, a church which had conformed so fully to the materialism and social prejudices of the day, should oppose the Wesleys, who set no store by money, held all men equal before God, and felt a mission to the "lower orders." Small wonder that almost every episcopal charge between 1740 and the end of the century attacked them; and even the most respectable descended to subtler practices. Thus, the great Bishop Gibson of London, whom Sir Robert Walpole called "the Pope of England and a very good Pope too," issued an anonymous pamphlet in 1743 which was much copied by his brethren. His main complaints were: first, that the Methodists set a standard of religion so high that some would be led to disregard religion altogether, and second, that this exalted strain of religion led men into the sin of contempt for their superiors.

There were several high-minded bishops, men like Bishop Butler who, even if they partook of plurality and absenteeism, did attend assiduously to the affairs of his diocese. Such men were not blind to the state of their times. Yet these men, no less than their more venal brethren, were opposed to Wesley almost to a man. How is this to be explained?

If Butler is taken as an example, the answer can be given with some precision. Undoubtedly he had had complaints from his clergy of the crowds who flocked to hear Wesley. Certainly he had heard of—and disapproved of—some of the scenes with which Wesley was confronted in the early days in Bristol. He had also heard certain false rumors, which Wesley was able to deny. And it seems clear that he was enough the captive of society to be alarmed at the idea of the gospel being preached in the open air to the colliers of Kingswood, even though he had no plans of how to reach them with the gospel himself. But perhaps he came closest to what he—and other bishops—felt in his famous remark that "to pretend to special revelations or gifts of the Holy Spirit was a horrid thing, a very horrid thing."

Here he hinted at an illuminism, which was far from Wesley's belief or practice. Bishop Gibson put it more plainly when he asked the Methodists to show what divine commission they have "when they tell us of extraordinary communications they have with God, and more than ordinary assurances of a special Presence with them; when they talk the language of those who have a special and immediate commission from God; when they profess to think and act under the immediate guidance of a divine inspiration." The Bishop of Lichfield, in his *Charge Against Enthusiasm*, published in 1744, aimed to prove that "the indwelling and inward witnessing of the Spirit in believers' hearts, as also the praying and preaching by the Spirit, are extraordinary gifts and operations of the Holy Ghost, belonging only to the apostolical and primitive times, and that consequently all pretensions to such favours in these last days are vain and enthusiastical." "The exigencies of the Apostolic Age re quired such miraculous gifts of the Spirit," wrote the bishop, "but there is no further occasion for them."

The impression one gets is that these men had no experience of the action of the Holy Spirit in their lives or surroundings — and so branded as illuminism the exaggerated version they chose to give of the action of the Spirit through the Wesleys. Having been on the defensive so long — "the *Analogy* exhibits religion on its last line of defence," says Temperley — they did not conceive that Christianity could go on the offensive. They seemed unable — or unwilling — to grasp that the Holy Spirit might possibly have new ways to meet the desperate needs of their age, needs they admitted but did little to meet. They recognized that the Spirit worked in "apostolical times," but strove to keep it quiet in their own day. The faintest whiff of that Spirit which bloweth where it listeth alarmed them as a breach of ecclesiastical order — and of episcopal slumbers. Meanwhile they went on efficiently practicing a method that did not work — and often did their best to hinder those who were trying, however imperfectly, to find a better one.

NINE
Schism and Rebirth

Wesley remained at heart a loyal son of the Church of England. Neither the persecution of Bishops nor the petty slights of lesser men deflected him. When, in 1742, Romilly, the curate at Epworth, refused his offer either to preach or even to read the prayers while he preached, Wesley cheerfully accepted the matter and spoke to a large audience standing on his father's tombstone. Next year when he visited Ep-worth, Romilly sent him the message: "Tell Mr. Wesley I shall not give *him* the Sacrament; for he is not *fit*." Wesley noted in his diary, "How wise a god is our God! There could not have been so fit a place under heaven, where this should befall me first, as my father's house, and the very place where 'according to the straitest sect of our religion' I had so long 'lived a Pharisee.' It was also fit in the highest degree that he who repelled me from that very table where I had myself so often distributed the bread of life, should be one who owed his all in this world to the tender love which my father had shown to his, as well as personally to himself."

Wesley founded his societies to provide care and discipline for those who had been awakened whether they were church people, nonconformists, or from the great masses who had

nothing to do with any church. He would have been happy
if the whole task could have been left to parish priests; but
felt there was a danger in putting live chicks under dead
hens. And there were other considerations. In 1757, Mr.
Walker of Truro—a clergyman who was constantly re-
questing Wesley to disband his preachers and rely upon the
clergy—wrote asking Wesley to forbid his itinerants to visit
the Methodist society in the parish of a Mr. Vowler. Now
Mr. Vowler was not a dead hen. Wesley had heard him
preach "two such thunderous sermons as he had scarce heard
these twenty years" and yet he did not feel able to comply
with Walker's suggestions. "I do not know that everyone
who preaches the truth has wisdom and experience to guide
and govern a flock," he wrote to Walker. "I do not know
whether Mr. Vowler could or would give that flock all the
advantages of holiness they now enjoy, and to leave them
to him before I am assured of this would be neither justice
nor mercy."

"From the first," Knox writes, "Wesley strikes you as a
man determined to create a weapon." He contrasts Wesley's
making of this weapon with Whitefield's "weaving a rope
of sand," and adds: "When Wesley died, he left behind a
powerful religious body, Anglican in inspiration, and for the
most part in membership, but ripe for schism." Certainly,
Wesley did aim to create a weapon, a weapon of the Holy
Spirit to "reform the nation." But this does not mean that
he was out to create a church. His concern was to raise up
a spiritual leaven, a salt which had not lost its savor. This
is why he so boldly and constantly removed those who
"walked unruly." It was not that he lacked pity for them.
He just felt their place was not in the *vanguard* of the
church's army, and that he could no longer suffer them to
hold up that advance. All his work presupposed the existence
of the church, and schism was never in his intention.

In starting his societies, Wesley did not think of himself as founding a church. He was following the precedent of other religious societies existing for the promotion of holiness within the Church of England at that time; there were thirty or forty in London, for example, in 1738. "We will not, dare not, separate from the Church," he wrote in 1766. "We are not seceders, nor do we bear any resemblance to them. We set out upon quite opposite principles. The seceders laid the very foundation of their work in judging and condemning *others*; we laid the foundation of our work in judging and condemning *ourselves*. They began everywhere, with showing their hearers, how fallen the *Church* and ministers are; we begin everywhere with showing our hearers how fallen they are *themselves*."

He goes on to direct that Methodist services be held at times differing from ordinary church services — preferably at five in the morning and five in the evening. "We never designed that our service should supersede church service," he continues. "Our service presupposes prayer, like the sermons at the University.[1] If it were designed to be instead of church service, it would be essentially defective; for it seldom has the four grand parts of public prayer; deprecation, petition, intercession, thanksgiving. Neither is it, even on the Lord's day, concluded with the Lord's Supper."

He concludes, "I advise all Methodists in England and Ireland, who have been brought up in the Church, constantly to attend the service of the Church, at least every Lord's day."

Wesley's great difficulty in holding to this course was to know how he was to care for those of his people who had previously had no church connection, or who had been refused communion by their parish priests. How was he to provide them with the sacrament? In the early years he and Charles alternated in the centers of London and Bristol, and by various means it was generally possible to keep a clergyman in each place. But the supply of clergy was very limited. Dr. Barnard, the Bishop of Londonderry, it is true, ordained Thomas Maxfield "to assist that good man that he may not work himself to death," but no other bishop would ordain men to help Wesley. John Jones, who assisted Wesley at the Foundry for some years, was ordained by a Greek Orthodox bishop, and it was only when Charles refused John's request to fill his place while he journeyed north, that John finally agreed for Jones to give the sacrament there. Societies all over the country were demanding that they be given the same advantages as the societies in London, and in 1760 three preachers in Norwich began to administer the sacra-ment. This thoroughly alarmed Charles who shot off letters in all directions demanding that they be banned. John was preaching in the North and quietly went on with his task.

The matter came up even more acutely twenty years later in America. In England there was a parish church wherever there was a Methodist society. In America this was not so. Clergymen were few and parish churches far distant from each other, and there were Methodist societies in many places where no church existed. Were the thousands of American Methodists, out of reach of churches, to be left without the sacraments? Or, were unordained Methodist preachers to administer them? This was the dilemma which faced John Wesley.

In 1746, Wesley had, while riding from London to Bristol, read *An Enquiry into the Primitive Church* by Peter King, and soon after Bishop Stillingfleet's *Irenicum*. He wrote to his brother: "Read Bishop Stillingfleet's *Irenicum* and I be-lieve you will think as I do. I verily believe I have as good a right to ordain, as to administer the Lord's Supper. But I see abundance of reasons why I should not use that right, unless I was turned out of the Church."

He had refused for over thirty years to act on his conviction. Even in 1780, he turned again to the Bishop of London, Dr. Lowth, in whose diocese America nominally was, and asked him to ordain men to care for the societies in America The Bishop refused and Wesley replied: "Your Lordship observes 'there are three ministers in that country already.' True, My Lord: but what are three to watch over all the souls in that extensive country? . . . Mr. Hoskins asked the favour of Your Lordship to ordain him, that he might minister to a little flock in America. Your Lordship did not see good to ordain him: but Your Lordship did see good to ordain and send to America other persons who knew something of Greek and Latin; but no more of saving souls than of catching whales." Wesley frankly told the Bishop that examining candidates in Greek and Latin was not as important as discovering "whether they serve Christ or Belial."

Even now Wesley did not ordain anyone for America. But the Revolutionary War created a new situation. Most of the Anglican clergy had either left America or had enlisted against the American people. So at the end of the war the Church of England was not recognized as a state church. Meanwhile, Wesley was faced with 15,000 American Methodists, many of whom had not received the sacraments for over a year, and with societies where scores of children had not been baptized for lack of a clergyman to do it. Consequently, in 1784, he at length ordained Dr. Coke with instructions to go to America and ordain the saintly Asbury, the two to be joint "superintendents" in America. "These are the steps," said Wesley, "which, not of choice, but necessity, I have slowly and deliberately taken. If anyone is pleased to call this separating from the Church, he may. But the law of England does not call it so; nor can anyone be properly said so to do, unless, out of conscience, he refuses to join in the service and partake of the Sacraments administered therein." In the same year, Wesley also—since his designated successor, Fletcher, was in bad health—had provided for the future of his work by appointing a Conference of a hundred men as his successors—the Legal Hundred—by Deed of Declaration lodged in the Court of Chancery. This was a more decisive step than the ordination of ministers in America, for it established a separate legal entity from the Church of England with its own unity and government. And in the next few years, Wesley also ordained ministers for Scotland and even three who were employed in England. In both cases he was moved by the urgent necessity to provide communion for those whom the church refused to admit; but from the legalistic point of view those were specific acts of disloyalty.

It has been held that ordination was the decisive step which Wesley took toward separation. This was certainly Charles' view. He believed with his old school friend Lord Mansfield that "ordination is separation." John stubbornly replied, "I see no use of you and me disputing together; for neither of us is likely to convince the other. You say I separate from the Church; I say I do not. Then let it stand."

In the years to come Charles was to prove more right than John on this point. Separation became a reality soon after John Wesley's death. But whether this was primarily John's fault—or the Church of England's—posterity can judge. Few today will dispute Archbishop Davidson's admission that the Primates of that era "were not the men to make the right response to a magnificent enthusiast like Wesley." Faced with the Bishops' noncooperation or worse,[2] Wesley had to choose between continuing his work at the expense of some of the laws of his beloved church or of keeping all her laws and stopping the work God had laid upon him. It was a frightful dilemma; and one which was not eased by Charles' lamentations.

Be that as it may, what does seem certain is that this man Wesley, so abused by the church leaders of his day, was the human instrument of that church's revival, even perhaps of its survival, in the succeeding century.

Historians of all schools of thought seem united in this assessment. J. R. Green, who claims that the Methodist revival "changed, after a time, the whole tone of English Society," states, "The Church was restored to new life and activity." Lecky, the rationalist, says that the Evangelicals, inspired by Wesley, "infused into the Church a new fire and passion of devotion, kindled a spirit of fervent philanthropy, raised the standard of clerical duty and completely altered the whole tone and tendency of the preaching of its ministers." The French historian, Halévy, adds: "We shall witness Methodism bring under its influence first the dissenting sects, then the Establishment, finally secular opinion. We shall explain by this movement the miracle of modern England, anarchist but orderly, practical and businesslike, but religious and even pietist." Seldom can Christ's word have become more appropriate to a mere man: that the stone which the builders had rejected became the head of the corner.

TEN
Trial by Wife

Dr. Johnson once remarked that Charles Wesley was "a more stationary man than his brother." This was not always so. In the tumultuous decade after 1739, the brothers alternated in the twin strongholds of Bristol and London and pursued each other in their strenuous, dangerous journeys through Cornwall, Ireland, and the North. In 1744, Charles spent the year in London, Bristol, Cornwall, Staffordshire, York-shire, Lincolnshire, Newcastle, Nottingham, and intervening places. In 1746 he was four months in London, six in Bristol and the West country, and the rest in the North. In 1748, the year before his marriage, he spent six months in Ireland.

Unlike John, Charles did not read on his journeys — in fact, as the years went on he read less and less except the Bible — but he composed hymns. The most serious effect of his fall from a horse near Ripley in 1743 was that it "spoiled my making hymns till the next day." He shared John's burning love of the poor and suffering, and also his courage, though Charles' was perhaps of a more pugnacious variety, derived like much of his character from his father. He was better known in his day for his preaching than his hymn-writing, and he had the same winning personality as his brother.

Riding into Bristol in September 1740, he was met by an army of more than a thousand Kingswood colliers on their way to cause a riot in the city. They were wild, desperate men, commonly considered to be murderers, heathen brutes, beyond the touch of church, charity, or instruction. Yet such was the force of Charles' presence and such was the affection in which he was held, that many turned back with him to Kingswood, while the rest conducted an orderly protest to the city fathers. "Like a flaming seraph," Tyerman says of this period, Charles "glowed with sacred love and music; and no toil, no danger or persecution was too great to be encountered."

By 1757, however, Charles had almost ceased to travel. Berridge put this down to his happy marriage in 1749 to Sally Gwynne, the pretty daughter of a Welsh landowner and the possessor of a lovely voice. "No trap so mischievous to the field preacher as wedlock," Berridge commented to Lady Huntingdon. "Matrimony has quite maimed poor Charles and might have spoiled John and George, if a wise Master had not graciously sent them a brace of ferrets." Certainly, Charles became more "stationary" after marriage. Sally had promised to allow him to continue traveling and had dissuaded her mother from exacting a promise, before marriage, that he would no more go to Ireland. Yet he never did set foot in Ireland again.

Charles' impending marriage had caused quite a stir. His brother had, six years earlier, written *Thoughts on Marriage and Celibacy*, a pamphlet in which he maintained that, although people could be as holy married as single, nevertheless the happy few with the power to abstain from marriage were "free from a thousand nameless domestic trials, and especially from the greatest of all entanglements, the loving of one creature above all others." So, he argued, they could devote all their time, money, and attention to God. "We may safely say," John concluded, "blessed are they who abstain from things lawful in themselves, in order to be more devoted to God."

In June 1749, this pamphlet had come up for review before the Conference, and John noted in his journal: "In a full and friendly debate my brethren convinced me that a believer might marry without suffering loss to his soul." So in the following April, John himself married Charles to Sally at Garth, and Charles entered in his diary: "We were cheerful without mirth, serious without sadness; and my brother seemed the happiest person amongst us."

Meanwhile, John himself had been contemplating matrimony—indeed his own determination seems to have predated his brethren's persuasions on his pamphlet. In August 1748, he had had a fever in Newcastle and been nursed by Grace Murray, a fascinating widow of thirty-two who after a stormy youth, marriage, conversion, and widowhood, was playing a prominent part in the Methodist headquarters there. When John was somewhat recovered he proposed marriage to her. She replied: "This is too great a blessing for me; I can not tell how to believe it. This is all I could have wished under heaven!" From that time Wesley regarded her as his fiancée. When he left Newcastle, she traveled with him into Derbyshire, where Wesley left her with another of her former patients, John Bennett, one of the few scholars among his itinerants. Imagine his astonishment, a few days later, when he received a letter from Grace and Bennett asking his permission that they should marry.

The story of the agonizing year that followed has often been told. Whenever Grace was near Wesley she pledged him her undying love. Whenever she was with Bennett she loved only him. Once Grace traveled to Ireland with Wesley and he noted: "She was to me both servant and friend, as well as fellow labourer in the Gospel; she provided everything I wanted and told me with all faithfulness and freedom, if she thought anything amiss in my behaviour. The more we conversed together, the more I loved her." Yet she was soon back with Bennett. No doubt she was flattered and bewildered to be between two such forceful and talented men.

Finally, in October 1749, the matter came, through a letter from John, to Charles' ears. He hurtled to horse, and did not rest until he had carried Bennett and Grace off to Newcastle, reconciled them, and discredited his brother by a mixture of deception, fury, and common sense. He did not leave Grace and Bennett until he had seen them married.

Tyerman's verdict on the affair is crisp, if over-simple: "John Wesley was a dupe. Grace Murray was a flirt. John Bennett was a cheat. Charles Wesley was a sincere, but irritated, impetuous and officious friend." Cownley, a friend of all and Bennett's confidant in the affair, said: "If Grace consult her ambition she will marry Mr. Wesley; if she consult her love she will marry Bennett," and this may not have been far from the truth.

Charles' intervention was well-meaning, and may have been well-judged, but his reasons for such intervention were many, and mixed. He believed that Grace was first promised to Bennett and that John's good name would not survive his "stealing" her—though when he told the Newcastle society that "if John is not damned there is no God" he was going a queer way about saving his reputation. He was convinced that John would break up the societies if he married so much beneath him socially and—a strange argument from him—that marriage would curtail John's usefulness. There were also personal motives. He was irritated, as was natural, by being one of the last, lulled as he was in his own domestic cocoon in Bristol, to know of the attachment—and he seems also to have felt a stab of possessive fear that a wife might supplant him in first place in his brother's affections.

With an insensitivity reminiscent of old Samuel, he seemed quite unaware that he had bitterly hurt John. True, White-field brought them together in a touching scene, but Charles ever afterward felt that John had a lessened affection for him—and complained bitterly of it to all. It is hard to do a man a wrong and feel quite the same about him. John was indeed a little wary, but the evidence is that any coldness through the years was rather on Charles' side and was caused by unrecognized forces within himself.

John's character shines clearly through the whole affair. Three times he offered to give Grace up to Bennett and was only deterred when Grace pleaded: "I am determined by my conscience as well as by inclination to live and die with you." His disappointment was terrible, yet within a day of his hearing of the Bennetts' marriage he was preaching at Leeds. He at once went to Newcastle and faced down the calumnies Charles had spread about him, and within a fort-night he even went to help John Bennett in his work in Rochdale.

John only once commented on the affair to anyone. In this letter to a friend he wrote: "Since I was six years old I never met with such a severe trial as for some days past. For ten years God had been preparing a fellow labourer for me by a wonderful train of providences. Last year I was convinced of it; therefore I delayed not, but as I thought, made all sure beyond a danger of disappointment. But we were soon after torn asunder by a whirlwind. In a few months, the storm was over; I then used more precaution than before and finally told myself that the day of evil would return no more. But it too soon returned, the waves rose again since I came out of London. The whole world fought against me; but above all, my own familiar friends. Then was the word fulfilled, 'Son of man, behold, I take away from thee the desire of thine eyes with a stroke.' The fatal irrevocable stroke was struck on Tuesday last."

In addition, while riding between Leeds and Newcastle, he wrote, to unburden his mind, a poem called "A Short Account of the Whole." The manuscript, in his exquisite writing with its many abbreviations and the distortions from the horse's trot, still exists. In it there is no word of reproach for his brother. His pain is great:

> Oh Lord, I bow my sinful Head!
> Righteous are all Thy Ways with Man.
> Yet suffer me with Thee to plead,
> With lowly Reverence to complain:
> With deep, unutter'd Grief to groan
> O what is this that Thou hast done?

But he turns to face the future:

> Teach me from every pleasing Snare
> To keep the Issues of my Heart;
> Be Thou my Love, my Joy, my Fear!
> Thou my eternal Portion art.
> Be Thou my never-failing Friend,
> And love, O love me, to the End!

John Wesley in 1751 married Mrs. Vazeille. He seems to have done this because his previous reasons for marrying still seemed valid and because of the advice of his friends, Blackwell and Perronet. He took Mrs. Vazeille largely on trust, partly because they spoke well of her and partly because of some earlier praise from Charles. The choice was

disastrous. Whether Grace would have made him the companion he hoped, we cannot say, but there was never any
chance of Mrs. Vazeille doing so. Where Grace was brave,
adventurous, and used to hardship, she was a cultivated
woman of "sorrowful spirit" and indifferent temper, a worthy
enough wife for some, but totally unsuited to the privations
and energies of Wesley's life. One can feel sympathy for her,
tied to the tail of John's comet, and finding that marriage
had brought her not worldly advancement, but the alter-
natives of constant travel or continual parting. She tried
both, before departing—but it can only be said that she did
all she could to make his life a misery. He treated her with
singular gentleness and good humor, even when she dragged
him across the room by his hair. His touch with his female
workers caused her much jealousy and finally she published
letters and even concocted some to try and ruin his reputation.

Even this did not ruffle him. When this matter came to
light John was planning to take Charles' daughter, Sally, on
a trip to Canterbury. Charles, hearing of it, became much
excited and urged John to cancel his journey. John was as
calm as his brother was agitated. Sally related years after,
"I shall never forget the manner in which my father accosted
my mother on his return after that talk. 'My brother,' said
he, 'is indeed an extraordinary man. I placed before him the
importance of the character of a minister and the evil con-
sequences which must result from his indifference to it, and
urged him by every relative and public motive to answer
for himself and stop the publication.' His reply was, 'Brother,
when I devoted to God my ease, my time, my life, did I
except my reputation? No. Tell Sally I shall take her to
Canterbury tomorrow.'"

One cannot say whether a happy marriage would, as
Berridge believed, have dulled John's commitment. An un-

happy one certainly did not. He wrote in his diary in 1751 —
perhaps thinking of his brother — "I cannot understand how
a Methodist preacher can answer to God, to preach one
sermon, or travel one day less in a married than in a single
state. In this respect surely, 'it remaineth that they who
have wives be as though they had none.'" Certainly John
practiced this throughout his life not only in his unhappy
marriage but in every turmoil and every temptation. Looking
at his life one cannot help feeling that his commitment would
have been equal to the subtler temptations of married con-
tentment.

Charles, on the other hand, became more and more stationary. After 1756 he only preached in Bristol and London.
He continued to pour out his hymns, but no longer necessarily
attended the annual Conference. He took no responsibility
for finance or the steady care of the preachers nationally, but
more and more confined himself to protesting at things of
which he disapproved. Thus, in 1763 he wrote violently
criticizing his brother for not being firmer with the enthusiasts, Bell and Maxwell. But when John asked him to come
up to London and help him in this crisis, he was unmoved.
"The sooner you could be here the better, for the mask is
thrown off," writes John to Charles on February 8. On the
26th he writes again, "I say no more about your coming to
London. Here I stand; and I shall stand, with or without
human help, if God is with us." In the following year John
implored Charles to come to London to fill his place in
administering communion while he took his necessary journey
to the North. Charles refused, at the same time objecting
to John Jones, the only other man available, officiating in his
place. John wrote to him on March 1, 1764, "You have
'no thoughts of venturing to London before May!' Then I
must indeed 'do the best I can.' So I must comply with the
advice of the stewards as well as my own judgement, and

insist upon John Jones assisting me on Sunday. I have delayed all this time out of tenderness to you. Adieu! John Wesley."

Various reasons have been given for Charles' inaction. He was certainly worried by the growing tendency among the preachers toward separation from the Church of England. But John did not wish this, and as he said: "Perhaps if you had kept close to me, I might have done better." Charles' health, too, was not good — but actually it thrived on action. The fact is that Charles had become less militant — and with loss of militancy, as is so often the case, had come criticism, and with criticism ill health and depression.

It is difficult to deny that Charles' inaction was tied up with his marriage. All his life he had sought dependence on others — first on his brother Samuel, then on John and for his last forty years upon his much loved wife, Sally. During his most active years, when each day was dangerous and the scene of action was large, this dependent quality in Charles was balanced by his conscious need of God and the resulting outpouring of God's power. But after marriage he found himself cramped into a kindly box. He found he had married Sally's family as well as Sally. Her sister, Becky, moved in with them; their closest woman friend moved to be near them, and music, the passion of the Gwynnes, became the center of their home.[1] Sally became ever dearer to Charles, but because of his over-dependence on her, he did not find in marriage those "unruffled days" which he had expected. He became fretful and depressed. His commitment had shrunk under the impact of domestic peace and affection. John was well aware of the situation, even though he appreciated Sally himself. "If I ventured to give you advice more," he wrote to Charles once, "it would be this: Be master in your own house. If you fly, they will pursue. But stand firm, and you will carry the point."

Charles' unresolved dependence on John had other unfortunate repercussions. He showed almost spiteful disloyalty to John in conversations with people like the Bennetts and Lady Huntingdon, while being scandalized when they echoed his criticisms. And even when Bennett, moved by a bit-terness deeper than he admitted or Charles recognized, black-guarded John and worked against him, Charles never glimpsed his responsibility in the matter.

That Charles continued, through his hymns especially, to make a great contribution to the awakening can not be denied. He was, perhaps, the greatest hymn-writer of all time, and no one without a deep and continuing Christian experience could have written as he did. Also, it must be remembered that he for sixteen years braved the dangers of the road as tirelessly and as fearlessly as John. John, moreover, was not guiltless in accepting Charles' dependence. Having accepted it when it applied to himself, it was not easy to cure when it became attached to Sally.

At this time, in January 1752, a curious document was signed by John, Charles, and nine others of the leading preachers. Written out in John's neat hand, and embodying principles as sound today as when they were written, it reads:

"It is agreed by us whose names are underwritten:
1. That we will not listen or willingly inquire after any Ill concerning each other.
2. That if we do hear any Ill of each other, we will not be forward to believe it.
3. That, as soon as possible, we will communicate what we hear, by speaking or writing, to the Person con-cerned.
4. That till we have done this, we will not write or speak a Syllable of it to any other Person whatever.

5. That neither will we mention it, after we have done this, to any other Person.

6. That we will not make any Exception to any of these Rules unless we think ourselves absolutely obliged in Conference so to do."

ELEVEN
The Don and the Peerage

Like Shakespeare, writes Knox, Wesley was not a solitary peak but the summit of a mountain range. Among kindred spirits who swayed the age were many mighty preachers. Besides brother Charles and George Whitefield, there were Fletcher, Venn and Grimshaw, Ingham, Romaine and Madan, besides Howel Harris in Wales, and the younger men like Toplady and Rowland Hill. And although John was by far the greatest influence among them, he was not really their leader, nor even their principal rallying point. Almost all of them, in his middle and later years, were at issue with him on predestination, and the person who had closer touch with them all than anyone else was a woman, Selina, Lady Huntingdon.

Lady Huntingdon was first converted through Ingham, one of the Holy Club at Oxford, and was with the Wesleys in that first society at Fetter Lane. Probably she was one of the minority who walked out with John and Charles on that evening when it was clear that the Moravians had taken it over — and when a sly Moravian spoiled John's exit by hiding his hat.

She saw herself in a double role. As her biographer states:

"On the week-days her kitchen was filled with the poor of the flock and on the sabbath the rich and noble were invited to spend the evening in her drawing room."

Her biographer has made her an easy target for sarcasm, for when a modern man reads of ladies "amiably condescending to their inferiors, even to the poorest," he is apt to erupt. "See what it was to be well-bred and religious at the same time," comments Vulliamy tartly. "If they had not listened to Mr. Ingham, these 'exalted females' might never have acquired the lovely merit of condescension!" But such reactions should not obscure the real courage of the woman. It was no light thing to sponsor the Methodist preachers among the *beau monde* of the day.

She certainly had courage. When Archbishop Cornwallis gave balls and routs at Lambeth Palace and Mrs. Cornwallis amazed the world by her extravagance, she went to court and complained personally to the King. The King sent a sharp letter to the Archbishop and remarked: "I wish there was a Lady Huntingdon in every diocese." To her own "spiritual routs" she invited everyone. And some responded. The formidable Sarah Jennings, Duchess of Marlborough, wrote: "Your concern for my improvement is very obliging. . . . God knows we all need mending, and none more than myself. . . . Women of wit, beauty and quality cannot bear too many humiliating truths — they shock our pride. But we must die; we must converse with earth and worms." Lord Dartmouth and the Earl of Buchan were among those who became identified with Methodism, while many others came to hear Whitefield in her chapels at Bath, Brighton, and Tunbridge Wells. Certainly, her action was to make the work of Wilberforce and his friends easier in the last years of the century.

Whitefield was her special favorite, but she maintained Venn, Romaine, Madan, and even Charles Wesley as her chaplains, and the gentle Fletcher was named president of her training college at Trevecca. Sometimes she would travel through the country attended by several of them, with all the trappings of a great lady. There is some truth in Knox's word that the only preachers who wrote her "with no hint of approaching her on all fours" were John himself, and the forthright Berridge of Everton.

One can readily believe that John did not fawn on Lady Huntingdon. His tone with "the great" was courteous, but firm. When, for example, he heard in 1764 that Lord Dartmouth had been turned from him by the whisperings of Lady Huntingdon, he wrote to Dartmouth:

Have not the objections you have heard made some impression on your lordship? Have they not occasioned, if I may speak freely, your lordship's standing aloof from me? Why do I ask? Indeed, not on my own account. . . . I can truly say, I neither fear nor desire anything from your Lordship. To speak a rough truth, I do not desire any intercourse with any persons of quality in England. I mean, for my own sake. They do me no good; and I fear, I can be none to them. . . .

Were I not afraid of giving your Lordship pain I would speak yet still further. Methinks you desire I should; that is, to tell you, once for all, every thought that arises in my heart. I will then. At present I do not want you; but I really think you want me. For, have you a person in all England who speaks to your Lordship so plain and down-right as I do? who considers not the Peer, but the man? not the Earl, but the immortal soul? who rarely commends, but often blames, and perhaps would do it oftener if you desired it? who is jealous over you with a godly jealousy, lest you should be less of a Christian by being a nobleman? lest, after having made a fair advance towards heaven, you should measure back your steps to earth again. O my Lord, is not such a person as this needful to you in the highest degree? If you have any such, I have no more to say, but I pray God to bless him to your soul. If you have not, despise not even the assistance which it may please God to give you by,

> My Lord,
> Your Lordship's ready servant,
> John Wesley.

If Dartmouth, who at least had the courage to stand with the Methodists, had also stuck closer to Wesley, he might have been more effective in the momentous tasks which were to meet him in the next decade. As Colonial Secretary and the step-brother of the Prime Minister, Lord North, at the beginning of the dispute with the American colonists, he occupied one of the key positions of the age. He was, writes Christie, "a mild and ineffective figure, liberal and sympathetic by temperament, but too soft and amiable to grapple effectively with problems of Government." He, like the rest of the Cabinet, was not to decide until it was too late whether to follow a policy of rigorous repression or of active conciliation—and he did not seem to have the quality to pursue either policy successfully. Wesley was to show in his letters in 1775 that he had a political and military foresight superior to that of both North and Dartmouth—and, certainly, they could have profited from a dash of his resolution as well as of his ability to change difficult men.

Some think that if Wesley had been a little more civil—or subservient—to Lady Huntingdon, if, for example, he had adopted the same attitude as that of George Whitefield, the split in the movement might have been averted. For it was Whitefield's favor with that noble lady that won her patronage for the Calvinist preachers, and it was her finance and generalship which propelled them through the country. While Whitefield lived, the split was avoided through the immense respect in which Wesley and Whitefield held each other. Wesley preached against predestination, but he would never attack Whitefield personally. "You may read a pamphlet against Mr. Wesley by Mr. Whitefield," he once said. "But you will never read a pamphlet against Mr. Whitefield by Mr. Wesley." Whitefield always thought of John as his master and mentor. He might write or preach against him one day even by name; but the next he would be seeking reconciliation with him whom he always called "Honoured Sir." "Never were theologians so resolved to make a molehill out of a mountain," says Knox.

After Whitefield died the whole Calvinist wing, with Lady Huntingdon in the van, moved more and more into opposition. The scandalous pamphlets of a Toplady and the snipings of "My Lady's preachers" tried Wesley sore. Yet in the perspective of two hundred years it is possible to say that there was a larger unity than they knew. These men together turned the tide of their age. Their disagreements were born in vigor and front-line faith, and were more vital — and seemingly more blessed of God — than the lazy agreements of Christians who have lost the hope and purpose to win the world.

TWELVE
Pope John's Rule

Was John Wesley an autocrat? His enemies — and some of his friends — called him "Pope John" in his lifetime, and there is no doubt that he was a man of strong will and personality. He did not easily give up his point of view. Knox, while thinking him pretty much of an autocrat, says that he generally won his point by "talking people round." One day, the Conference would decide a thing one way — in a sense contrary to Mr. Wesley's opinion — and two days later they would quietly and unanimously decide just the opposite!

Wesley did occupy a position of great ascendancy. For consider his situation: by 1765 Charles was virtually retired; Whitefield was an invalid with asthma and mostly working with Lady Huntingdon; Grimshaw was dead and most of the other clergymen were settled in parishes. John Newton, the ex-slave-ship-captain who was later to play a major part in converting William Wilberforce, was typical of those who sympathized with Wesley, but would not join him because they regarded the itinerant life as too costly. Fletcher, who, after Grimshaw's death, was designated by Wesley as his successor, proved less durable than the indestructible John, and was an invalid long before his death in 1785. Before that he had retired into a parish, to John's sorrow, for he believed this saintly man to be "full as much called to sound an alarm through all the nation as Mr. Whitefield himself: Nay, abundantly more so, seeing he was far better qualified for that important work." Wesley was alone at the top, even though the surge of lay preachers continually grew. "With or without help, I creep on," he wrote to Charles.

John never ceased urging Charles to take a full part with him in the work. Thus in February 1766, he wrote, "Dear Brother, we must, we must, you and I at least, be all devoted to God! And then wives, and sons, and daughters, and everything else, will be real, invaluable blessings. . . . Let us this day use all the power we have! If we have enough, well; if not, let us this day expect a fresh supply. How long shall we drag on thus heavily, though God has called us to be the chief conductors of such a work? Alas! What conductors! If I am, in some sense, the head, and you the heart, of the work, may it not be said, 'The whole head is sick and the whole heart is faint'! Come, in the name of God, let us arise, and shake ourselves from the dust! Let us strengthen each other's hands in God, and that without delay. Have *senes sexagenarii* time to lose? Let you and I, and our house, serve the Lord in good earnest. May His peace rest on you and yours! Adieu! John Wesley."

And again in June of the same year, John wrote: "Dear Brother, I think you and I have abundantly too little intercourse with each other. Are we not old acquaintances? Have we not known each other for half a century? And are we not jointly engaged in such a work as probably no two other men upon earth are? Why then do we keep at such a distance? It is a mere device of Satan. But surely; we ought not, at this time of day, to be ignorant of his devices. Let us, therefore, make full use of the little time that remains. We, at least, should think aloud and use to the uttermost the light and grace on each bestowed, and insist everywhere on full redemption, receivable now by faith alone! Consequently to be looked for now. You are made as it were for this very thing. Just here you are in your element. In connection I beat you; but in strong, short-pointed sentences, you beat me. Go on, in what God has peculiarly called you to. Press the instantaneous blessing; then I shall have more time for my peculiar calling, in forcing the gradual work. We must have a thorough reform of the preachers. My love to Sally. John Wesley."

He never treated his brother Charles except as an equal. But he could not share leadership of the work with people who would not undertake the same commitment. A leader of a spiritual revolution cannot be elected. He can only commit himself. And only similarly committed men can take the full lead with him. Such men were few and far between as the years went on. Many took on a part; many sacrificed everything; but few took on the whole weight which lay on Wesley's back and which increased with the years.

Wesley spoke of his situation at the Conference of 1766. He explained how the work had grown naturally. People and then preachers had gathered around him and asked him to direct them. He had complied. "Now several gentlemen are much offended at my having so much power. My answer to them is this: I did not seek any part of this power. It came upon me unawares. But when it was come, not daring to bury that talent, I used it to the best of my judgement. Yet I never was fond of it. I always did and do now, bear it as my burden; the burden which God lays upon me; but if you can tell me anyone, or any five men, to whom I may transfer this burden, who can and will do just what I do now, I will heartily thank both them and you."

He said that some considered this to be "shackling freeborn

Englishmen" and demanded a free conference — that is a meeting of all the preachers where all things should be determined by a majority vote. "I answer it is possible after my death something of this kind may take place, but not while I live. To me the preachers have engaged themselves to submit to serve me as sons in the Gospel. But they are not thus engaged to any man or number of men besides. To me the people in general will submit; but they will not submit to any other. It is nonsense then to call my using this power 'shackling free-born Englishmen.' None needs to submit to it unless he will, so there is no shackling in this case. Every preacher and every member may leave me when he pleases; but when he chooses to stay, it is on the same terms that he joined me at first."

In maintaining this, Wesley had in mind his original aim of founding not a church, but societies within the church. He was out to "spread scriptural holiness" by means of the leaven of his private and personal societies. Thus, when he expelled people for "walking disorderly" — whether it was for persistent smuggling or for immorality or for name-calling — he was not excommunicating people, but preserving his leaven. The expellees had the broad bosom of the established church to cushion their fall. It was much the same personal view of his societies which he was explaining to his preachers.

On the other hand, Wesley always desired correction from others and sought it. "Nothing can be more kind than the mentioning of what you think is amiss in my conduct," he wrote to a difficult clergyman. "The more freedom you use in doing so, the more I am indebted to you." On another occasion Wesley was having breakfast at City Road, as was customary on Sunday mornings, with his itinerant and local preachers. One young man rose during breakfast and found fault with one of his seniors. Thomas Rankin was furious and sharply rebuked the young man for his impertinence; but in turn was rebuked by Wesley. "I will thank the young-est man among you to tell me of any fault you see in me," he said to those assembled. "In doing so I shall consider him my best friend." "No man in England has contradicted me as much as you have done, Henry," said Wesley on another occasion to Henry Moore. "And yet, Henry, I love you still. You are right."

There were times, as with the case of John MacNab in 1779, when things did get out of hand, but in general it may be said that Wesley led because he loved the most, suffered the most, and was manifestly called to do so by God. He was led by the Spirit, and that was why others willingly allowed him to lead them. If there was a fault, it was that he did not find a way of curing the character defects in a man like Charles which caused him to withdraw. In old age, looking over his correspondence, John was able to say that he had never left any of those companions who had been closest to him, but some had left him. The art of raising up men, under God, who can do what you do better than you do it yourself is the most difficult in every sphere of leadership — and most difficult of all in the spiritual realm.

THIRTEEN
The Loyal
Revolutionary

Wesley was a mighty social force in his own lifetime. As the Englishman who spoke to more of his countrymen face to face than any other man of his century, as one of the widest read pamphleteers of his age, and, above all, as the undisputed head of a compact body of militant people, his opinions were greatly regarded. "For universality of influence," writes the *Cambridge Modern History*, "he had no rival." "No man lived nearer the centre than John Wesley, neither Pitt nor Clive, neither Mansfield nor Johnson," wrote Augustine Birrell. "You cannot cut him out of the national life. No single figure influenced so many minds, no single voice touched so many hearts."

He tackled certain social evils direct. His pamphlet against the slave trade—"that execrable sum of all the villainies"—issued in 1774, was one of the first denunciations to reach a wide public; and his last letter, written on his deathbed, was to Wilberforce, urging the young liberator on in his battle against the trade. He set his face against smuggling—4,500 horses were engaged in this occupation in Suffolk alone—and against gin stills which Lecky called the "master curse of the age." He was against the abuse of the under privileged and for the relief and education of the poor. He also denounced corruption both in India and in British political life, with his usual straightforward pithiness.

Wesley did not intervene in party politics. But in all the crises of the century — the '45, the threats of French and Spanish invasion, the American Revolution — he was a force for stability, although often accused of being just the opposite. As the dispute with the American colonies began to brew, he wrote to Charles: "I am of neither side, and yet of both; on the side of New England, and of old. . . . Love all and pray for all with a sincere and impartial love." A few weeks later he is writing to the Prime Minister, Lord North, one of his intensely practical letters. "In spite of my long-rooted prejudice," he said, referring to his Tory opinions, "I cannot avoid thinking that an oppressed people asked for nothing more than their legal rights and that in the most modest and inoffensive manner that the nature of the thing would allow. These men will not be frightened: they will probably dispute every inch of ground, and if they die, die sword in hand." To Lord Dartmouth, the Colonial Secretary and the only man in the Cabinet actively touched by Methodism, he pointed out that the Americans were fighting for their homes, not for pay, and, unlike the British nation, were united. He also predicted that France and other nations would join in, at a time when many Britons were "ripe for rebellion" — a prediction that was to come true. "Remember Charles I," he ended.

But as the war progressed and the last chance of peaceful settlement seemed past, as other countries prepared to join in against Britain and subversion spread throughout the land, Wesley came out strongly for King and government, notably in a pamphlet which was an abridgement of Dr. Johnson's *Taxation no Tyranny.* He was soon lampooned as a government stooge, though he refused all government favor for himself when, for the only time in his life, it was offered to him.[1] "I know mankind too well," he commented at the time. "They who love you for political service, love you less than their dinner; and they that hate you, hate you worse than the devil."

Wesley's steadying hand in all the main crises of his times is, no doubt, one reason why historians like Lecky, Halévy, and Temperley have credited him with saving Britain from a revolution of blood, similar to that which overtook France in 1789. But it is only a small part of the tale. To most of Wesley's contemporaries, he seemed not conservative but revolutionary. He felt himself called to the poor and, unlike the parsons of his day, treated the virtues and sins of the outcast exactly the same as those of the privileged. This infuriated not just a Lady Buckingham or a Dr. Borlase, but the whole establishment. Moreover, he broke the monopoly of learning, and taught the poor to preach to and educate the poor. "This," writes Vulliamy, "was the culminating grievance. The idea of men in shabby clothes expounding the scriptures in a vulgar dialect was too horrible, if it was not too ridiculous. No one could profitably point the way to heaven unless he wore a surplice and knew the parts of a Latin verb when he saw them. It was a dastardly filching of prerogative. True, the first apostles were humble men; but things had changed enormously since the days of the apostles; everyone agreed that there could be no such thing as grace without education."

Curiously enough, these absurd protesters were right, not wrong, in their fears. Wesley would not have advocated universal suffrage nor did he favor Wilkes the libertine who nevertheless fought a key battle for political freedom. Yet Wesley's life and work presaged a coming revolution in social relationships. It is said that he gave working people a satisfaction which drew their minds away from physical revolution — and Charles' quelling of the riot of Kingswood colliers is quoted in support. More accurately it could be said that he provided a moral equivalent of revolution. He said that social change could only come through personal change, but that personal change was no change unless it resulted in social change. Today, people wanting to avoid the cost of personal change try to gather the fruit of change without planting the root experience. And the result is a materialism which defeats their best endeavors.

Tens of thousands of workers accepted change for themselves through Wesley and his friends. This restored to them their self-respect, for he taught them that spiritually they were the equals of "their betters." He gave them education and stimulated them to want it. Many learned their public speaking as lay preachers and learned to read through his Christian library. It was from such men, as Halévy has stressed, that the British Labor Movement sprang. Of the six Tolpuddle martyrs,[2] for example, five were Methodists, while the sixth caught a Methodist faith from them in prison. These men were ejected from their homes by parson and magistrates for their Methodist belief before they were arrested for their trade unionism. And the official historian of the agricultural worker writes, "They were honoured — perhaps too much as trade unionists, too little as men, men superior in every way to their persecutors."

Commentators from Halévy to the Webbs stress that it was such men who led the labor movement throughout the nineteenth century, a fact that was once more illustrated in the person of Keir Hardie himself who said, "I myself have found in the Christianity of Christ the inspiration which first drove me into the movement and which carried me on in it."

But if the change that Wesley advocated began first among the laboring classes, it took hold no less surely at the other end of society. It worked in Wilberforce, the friend of Pitt, and the others who abolished both slavery and the slave trade. It worked through Lord Shaftesbury and the other factory reformers; and Marx himself called the Factory Act of 1847 a turning-point in the workers' fight, while the Marxist historian, Rothstein, said that Lord Shaftesbury's movement "may be said to have saved the country from a revolution which seemed likely to break out at any moment." From men like Wilberforce and Shaftesbury a new spirit spread to their whole class. According to John Marlowe they "made heartlessness unfashionable" and their influence "remained to soften the harsh light of the Victorian governing class and acquisitiveness and to tone down the consequent bitterness of antagonism between class and class, until much of that which they had hoped to achieve by compassion expressed in personal service was at length in some sort achieved by the democratic process."

Halévy remarked this double action of "evangelical religion" when he called it the "moral cement" of nineteenth-century English society. It "restrained the plutocrats who had newly risen from the masses from vulgar ostentation and debauchery and placed over the proletariat a select body of workmen enamoured of virtue and capable of self-restraint. Evangelicalism restored to England the balance momentarily destroyed by the explosion of the revolutionary forces."

Harold Nicolson, in *The Age of Reason*, sums up: "Lecky goes so far as to state that it was Methodism which at the end of the eighteenth century preserved England from a revolution as terrible as that of France. Had it not been for this great movement to revival, the industrial revolution might have assumed even more dangerous shapes. Methodism, for the working classes, proved a welcome emotional sedative, while it gave to the rich a sense of responsibility and philanthropic conscience. It passed on to the evangelicals its high ideals of public and private duty; by its example it reformed and raised the Church of England; it purified politics, gave a fresh stimulus to public education, and created the wave of humanitarianism that led to the abolition of slavery and penal reform. Certainly it was one of the most civilizing inspirations that has ever improved the lot of man. All this was due to the genius and virtue of the gifted and charming little scholar who was born in Epworth Parsonage on 17 June 1703."

FOURTEEN
Regiments
of Reform

These profound social results were not achieved through a self-conscious social program, like that which sections of various denominations cultivate today. Wesley was not a political priest who, having lost the power to change men, set out to denounce other peoples or alter some secular program. Yet his social aim was a conscious one. It was the natural result of his passionately experienced faith — of what, today, we might call his ideology. For it is not true that ideologies are always materialistic or opposed to Christian faith. The materialistic ideologies of this and every age are the substitutes men find when they cease to live their faith with the passion, discipline, and thoughtful strategy which Jesus demonstrated and which the greatest of his followers have exemplified ever since. Wesley lived his Christianity in such a way that it possessed him totally and permeated every part of life, first for himself and then for thousands of others.

His way of working is well seen in his battle against slavery and the slave trade. First he faced the facts which the statesmen and churchmen of his country were determined to ignore. So in his *Thoughts Upon Slavery*, one of the first denunciations to reach a wide public, he gives a restrained, but grim picture of the horrors of slavery. Then he makes the moral test: "Can human law turn darkness into light, or evil into good?" "Notwithstanding ten thousand laws," he says, in the face of the three royal charters, the Act of Parliament and the two treaties which had legalized the trade, "right is right and wrong is wrong. . . . I absolutely deny all slave-holding to be consistent in any degree with even natural justice." "The whole business," he continues, is pursued "to get money," and its excuses are "empty and hypocritical." Sweeping away the appeals to economic necessity and to the supposed needs of defense, he adds: "I deny that villainy is ever necessary; a man can be under no necessity of degrading himself into a wolf!" And again: "It is better that all these islands [the British West Indies] should remain uncultivated for ever; yea, it were more desirable that they were all together sunk in the depth of the sea than that they should be cultivated at so high a price." "Never was anything such a reproach in England," he writes three years later, "as the having any hand in this execrable traffic. . . . Certain it is that England may not only subsist but abundantly prosper without them — may increase its population, agriculture, manufactures though it no more suck the blood and devour the flesh of the *less barbaric* Africans."

Having stated and restated the issue, Wesley went quietly on his way, changing men — for he believed that the shortest cut to reform was to charge other hearts with the same passionate faith which possessed his own. Overton, the church historian, speaks of this faith which "made selfish men self-denying, the discontented happy, the worldling spiritually minded, the drunkard sober, the sexual chaste, the liar truthful, the thief honest, the proud humble, the godless godly, the thriftless thrifty." Such men became the regiments of reform, and he trusted that in the same way leaders would be raised up who would be the generals in the decisive fight against the evil.

By the end of his life this had come to pass. William Wilberforce, Pitt's closest friend and one of the ablest men in the Commons, was changed as an indirect result of Wesley's work. One day in 1787, Wilberforce wrote in his journal: "God Almighty has set before me two great objects, the suppression of the slave trade and the reformation of the morals of England." Wesley, now nearing his end, recognized the young Member of Parliament as the man raised by God to complete the work. Six days before he died, the last letter he ever wrote was a clarion call which was to inspire Wilberforce all his life. Wesley wrote:

My dear Sir,

Unless the Divine Power has raised you up to be as Athanasius, *contra mundum*, I see not how you can go through your glorious enterprise in opposing that execrable villainy which is the scandal of religion, of England, and of human nature. Unless God has raised you up for this very thing, you will be worn out by the opposition of men and devils; but *if God be for you, who can be against you?* Are all of them together stronger than God? Oh, *be not weary in well doing.* Go on, in the name of God and in the power of His might, till even American slavery, the vilest that ever saw the sun, shall vanish away before it.

Reading this morning a tract wrote by a poor African, I was particularly struck by that circumstance that a man who has a black skin, being wronged or outraged by a white man, can have no redress; it being a *law* in our colonies that the oath of a black against a white goes for nothing. What villainy is this!

That He who has guided you from your youth up,
  may continue to strengthen you in this and in all things,
  is the prayer of,

Dear Sir,
Your affectionate servant,
John Wesley.

Years of struggle lay ahead. But in 1807 the Commons carried
Wilberforce's motion abolishing the trade. And twenty-six
years later Wilberforce was to hear on his deathbed that the
House had voted twenty million pounds sterling to effect
the abolition of slavery within the year.

FIFTEEN
Who Was for Freedom?

In Wesley's day, as in our own, new and vivid ideas were at large in Europe. He was born nine years after Voltaire and nine years before Rousseau, the principal literary creators of the French Revolution. They both died in 1778 and were reburied, side by side, in the Panthéon in 1791. "He taught us to be free" was the proud legend inscribed by the painter David on Voltaire's hearse. It was a sentiment which thousands of ordinary Englishmen were even then saying of Wesley, who died in that same year.

Voltaire and Rousseau were the great exponents of a religion which is still with us today. "If Voltaire was the creator of the religion of man," writes Isaiah Berlin, "Rousseau was the greatest of its prophets." This religion, says Berlin, "emphasized the natural goodness of man unspoiled by a bad or ignorant government, and the immense power of rational education to rescue the masses of mankind from present miseries, to institute a juster and more scientific distribution of the world's goods and so to lead humanity to the limits of attainable happiness."

Voltaire was a destructive writer of genius. With the flame of his irony and the blast of his sarcasm, he exposed shams and withered away "superstitions." "It was he who taught three generations that superstition was ridiculous, sentiment absurd, fanaticism unintelligent and oppression infamous." He believed that he had seen the victory of Reason in his lifetime. "It is certain," he wrote, "that the knowledge of nature, the sceptical attitude towards old fables dignified by the name of history, a healthy metaphysic freed from the absurdities of the schools, are the fruits of that century when reason was perfected." As positive policy he had little to offer, except a series of fierce campaigns to right individual acts of injustice. His lampooning of things which needed lampooning and his genuine hatred of injustice did not give a constructive philosophy to replace the world he was destroying.

Rousseau, on the other hand, was a preacher and a propagandist. He brought a new eloquence and ardor to the religion of man, a richer, more emotional appeal which thrilled the multitudes who, while agreeing with Voltaire's negatives, were somewhat tired of the arid rectitude of Reason, as so far presented. The *Contrat Social*, said H. A. L. Fisher, "struck France with the force of a new gospel. Rivers of revolutionary sentiment were released by the phrase 'Man was born free but is everywhere in chains.'" He developed the idea of the natural goodness of man to such lengths that he contended that "the People" could do no wrong. If an individual was opposed to the "General Will," then society had the right to "force him to be free" — a conception which was to come in handily and bloodily in the Revolution and was to be perpetuated as the "Dictatorship of the Proletariat" in our day.

Wesley's fundamental quarrel with Voltaire and Rousseau was not their vision of the corruption of eighteenth-century ruling classes — for, although a Tory by conviction, he was well aware of corruption in high places and was as opposed as they were to unreasoned superstitions. His disagreement was with their pathetic faith that men of themselves were good and would, left to themselves, create a just society. He knew that human nature, by itself, was inadequate — which made him prepare himself for his mission with long years of self-knowledge, discipline, and purification.

Neither Voltaire nor Rousseau felt the need of such a cleansing. Rousseau held that if one wanted to acquire a "perfect nature," one must give up all thought of being clever and aim only to be good. Yet Nicolson calls his character "despicable," and William James brands him "contemptible." He "inflamed all the mothers of France to follow nature and nurse their own babies themselves," says James, while depositing all his own five children on the steps of a foundlings' hospital.

Voltaire, with his wit and sensitiveness to injustice, was a more attractive figure. He nevertheless found time to amass a vast fortune for himself, by money-lending, currency-running, and speculation over army contracts, while much of the time living off his current mistress. His character is mercilessly revealed in his relationship with Frederick the Great, "a mutual infatuation which furnishes a perfect case history of the manner in which adulation can be degraded into subservience and subservience lead to venomous hatred." His shameless toadying to Frederick, and indeed to Catherine of Russia, was even more exaggerated than the attitude of some Western intellectuals to Stalin and Khrushchev in a later day.

"One of the two most startling aberrations in which the Age of Reason indulged," writes Nicolson, "was to take as its hero and its heroine two tyrants who, to our minds, violated all the principles by which reason should be judged and applauded. If we are to grasp how utterly unreasonable the Age of Reason really was, it is useful to examine what was felt at the time about their strange heroines and heroes. It is merely curious that they should have been taken in by such obvious charlatans as Saint-Germain, Cagliostro, and Casanova. What is to our minds almost incredible is that they should have continued to admire and applaud a feckless courtesan such as Madame de Pompadour, a murderess and adulteress such as Catherine II, and a bloodstained aggressor such as Frederick the Great."

Wesley, on the other hand, applied to himself the most exacting standards of discipline and morality, and received in due time the gift of that Spirit which made his character triumphant and winning. His principle and his knowledge of himself — never perfect, but far keener than that of a Voltaire — helped him to see men and events more clearly. He was not deceived by rank and wealth, for he wished nothing from such people. He was not out to please men, but God — which gave him a sovereign dignity and freed him from the twin errors of toadying and condemning.

Which was the most effective way?

We have already seen Wesley's effect upon the slave trade. To the honor of the French philosophers it must be said that they were among the first to question the morality of the slave trade. But it was men in Britain whose lives had been changed and possessed by the message which Wesley preached who actually abolished the trade — and so stimulated British diplomacy that it forced France, after the Napoleonic wars, to follow its lead.

And what of the freedom of which David wrote on Voltaire's hearse? The French Revolution, made in order to secure liberty, equality, and fraternity among men, changed the face of Europe, but failed in its objectives. Wesley's less dramatic revolution in the lives of tens of thousands of Englishmen, on the other hand, not only gave men that "perfect freedom" which is found in "His service," but resulted in

a crop of reforms which made the liberty of England her
greatest boast and asset in the succeeding century.

Voltaire had first learned his deism from Englishmen. The
fact that deism did not make as much progress in England
as in France was partly due to the fact that France produced
no Bishop Butler to tackle it with his superior intellect. But
Butler's philosophy could not grasp the working people of
England as Rousseau's thought gripped the French. To out-
match the fire of the French Revolution an equal fire was
needed. And this could only come through men who, like
Wesley, lived a passionate faith and took it to the nation.

SIXTEEN
End and Beginning

Wesley fought to the end. He attributed his vitality to early rising, plain diet, and horse-riding. He might have added that he had had a purpose so great that he had not worried about himself for over fifty years. For, as Overton wrote, "hardly a shadow of doubt about his spiritual state crossed his mind" from the time in 1739 when he accepted, against his will, in field-preaching, the commitment to pioneer a new way in England.

Charles died in 1788. All February and March 1788, he lay ill. John bombarded him and Sally with letters, urging on them the remedies he had found effective himself. "Dear Brother," he wrote on February 17, "You must go out every day or die. Do not die to save charges. You certainly need not want for anything as long as I live. John Wesley." He was referring to the hire of horse and carriage. He also prescribed "ten drops of elixir of vitriol in a glass of water" and, to ease pain in the stomach, "a large onion split across the grain and bound on the pit of the stomach." Meanwhile, John himself, eighty-five and as yet "feeling none of the infirmities of old age," was traveling thirty or forty miles a day.

John was outwardly unmoved by his brother's death. The obituary in the minutes of the 1788 Conference was terse, as John's writing always was when he felt most deeply. Only once did his iron control relax. Rising at Bolton, two weeks after his brother's death, to announce "Wrestling Jacob," Charles' great hymn which "Mr. Watts did not scruple to say was worth all the verses he himself had written." John read:

> Come, O Thou Traveller unknown,
> Whom still I hold, but cannot see.
> My company before is gone
> And I am left alone with Thee.

For the first time in his life he broke down in public. He sat down in tears and hid his face in his hands.

John was soon up again. That year he preached in almost every county in England and Wales. Next year he admitted that "he could not easily preach more than twice a day" and he had been annoyed, a little earlier, to find that he could no longer write for more than fifteen hours in the day without hurting his eyes. His own end came on March 2, 1791. He had preached his last sermon at Leatherhead on February 23, and written his great letter to Wilberforce from Balham on the 24th. Then he returned to City Road and there, surrounded by his friends, his battle ceased. Almost his last words were: "The best of all is God is with us."

During his closing years, Wesley had become an honored name in England. Persecution had ceased for him, if not for his men, and he was surprised and a little shocked to find the Bishop of London yielding precedence to him. Yet it was many decades before his life was seen in perspective — for, though he ceased, the effect of his life worked on in men's hearts, until many felt with Birrell that "no other man did such a life's work for England." And not for England only. At his death, there were already 42,265 members of Methodist societies in America, and by 1950 they had increased to around ten million. From America, as from England, his message spread everywhere until his prophetic words to fearful friends in 1739 had, indeed, become true. The world had become his parish.

As I write, there is a growing hope — a hope better founded than at any time since Wesley's death — that Methodism and the Church of England may reunite. As an Anglican married to a Methodist, I rejoice to see it. The way will not be easy, but all will be grateful to those who labor to achieve something so near to the Wesleys' own conception.

Yet, in the light of Wesley's heroic story, sharp questions spring to mind. Is reunion now a possibility, one wonders, because we of the Church of England are better people than, for example, Bishop Butler? Or is it just that we find it easier to repent of our ancestors' prejudices than of our own? Do we rise swiftly to assist and learn from the uncomfortable prophets of our own day?

Would we Anglicans, in fact, be as eager to accept reunion with the Methodists, if Methodism today were the scalding, effective, original force that it was in Wesley's lifetime? Has Methodism, perhaps, lost the quality to "sting" the establishment which made Bishop Gibson wish to expel it from the church's breast?

Above all, there is the deeper question: will reunion of itself renew the nation, as Wesley renewed it in his own day?

Few would pretend that Britain is less lost in materialism today than it was in the eighteenth century: indeed, this evil now seems dominant not just in a ruling class, but in the whole nation. Spiritual regeneration is possible, but it will not be achieved merely by two churches, each on the defensive, deciding to get together. The uniting of the three Methodist churches in 1932, admirable as it was, did not arrest their decline nor greatly influence the nation.

Wesley's secret was that he sought and found God's fresh ways of bringing reality to his generation. He did not pretend that nothing new was needed, nor did he water down Christ's commands into a "new morality" in an attempt to appeal to intellectuals or to court the young. He found reality for himself — and gave up ease, friends, and cherished opinions to take it to the whole nation. He forgot himself and worked at God's pace, not his own, until the very day he died: and he enjoyed every day of it.

What is the equivalent for Christians in our day and generation? One thing is certain: the right way will need efforts as arduous, and will bring opposition as bitter, as any that Wesley had to face. But the strong spirits of youth will rally to such a venture, so that men will say with Wesley: "For what pay would you procure men to do this service, to be always ready to go to prison or to death?"

NOTES

CHAPTER 1

1. Jeremy Taylor's *Holy Living* and *Holy Dying*, at this time, and William Law's *Christian Perfection* and *A Serious Call*, when they were published in 1726 and 1729, had an even deeper effect.
2. The distinction between Wesley's diaries and his journals is important. He published long extracts from his journals which were, in the main, written for publication, but he took elaborate precautions to protect the privacy of his diaries, which were written partly in cipher, partly in abbreviated longhand, and partly in shorthand.
3. Many authors identify Varanese with Betty Kirkham, but V. H. H. Green writes: "It can now be stated categorically that Varanese was Sarah Kirkham."
4. An offer quickly snapped up by another distant relative, who was an ancestor of the future Duke of Wellington. "Had Charles accepted," comments Lunn, "there might have been no Methodists and there would certainly have been no Iron Duke."

CHAPTER 4

1. A strange feature was that these phenomena happened only in Bristol and Newcastle—and attended Wesley's preaching more than that of the far more dramatic Whitefield or the more passionate Charles. Also, they became rarer as the Revival spread. In later life, Wesley was to doubt whether it was always "God confirming His word" and felt that it was often the Devil counterfeiting Him or making a final struggle for a man. These experiences owed little to the fear of hell—for Wesley laid no special emphasis there.
Rupert Davies writes in *Methodism* (Pelican 1963), "Modern psychological man is bound to look at such things in a different light. He will at once think of exhibitionism, mass hysteria, and other states with even more sinister names. Their presence . . . cannot be denied. But it has to be noted that Wesley's words were working on highly suggestible but not necessarily neurotic people;

he was saying things of tremendous import that they had never heard before, for their authorized pastors had neglected to teach them, and they were bound to be struck violently, both with dismay and with joy, as they thought first of their sins and then of God's incredible grace and mercy; and many, perhaps very many, of those who went through these shattering experiences continued for the rest of their lives in quiet and practical goodness. It may be that for them a sudden shock was the only, or the best, or at least a harmless way of appropriating divine truth."

CHAPTER 8

1. A. W. Rowden, *Primates of the Four Georges*, p. 167.
2. Edmund Pyle, *Memoirs of a Royal Chaplain*, 1729–63, p. 305.
3. A. W. Rowden, *Primates of the Four Georges*, p. 378.

CHAPTER 9

1. The Oxford University Sermon then, as now, was delivered at a different time from Matins and was accompanied by a minimum of prayer.
2. Bishop Gibson wrote in *Orthodoxy versus Methodism*: "Every prudent society must desire that they would withdraw from her bosom who by sheltering themselves in it can wound and sting her effectually."

CHAPTER 10

1. This was to come out in Charles' talented sons and even more talented grandson. The household moved to London to forward the children's musical education and their recitals to the aristocracy were, naturally, the parents' pride and joy.

CHAPTER 13

1. Wesley always regretted that he had not used the occasion to get himself offered a "royal mission" with the right to preach in all churches in the realm.
2. The Tolpuddle martyrs were the founders of the first British trade union.

CHAPTER 14

1. The story is told in my *Brave Men Choose*.

SELECTED
BIBLIOGRAPHY

These books were published in Great Britain, but for those that have American editions, the American publisher is listed.

The Journal of John Wesley, edited by Percy L. Parker. Chicago: Moody Press, 1974.

The Letters of John Wesley, edited by J. Telford. Epworth, 1931.

Works of John Wesley. Eleventh edition. London, 1856.

Abbey, Charles J. and Overton, John H. *The English Church in the Eighteenth Century*. New York: Scholarly Reprints, Inc., 1976.

Belden, A. D. *George Whitefield the Awakener*. Rockliff, 1953.

Berlin, Isaiah. *Karl Marx: His Life and Environment*. New York: Oxford University Press, 1963.

Brailsford, M. R. *A Tale of Two Brothers*. Hart-Davis, 1954.

Bready, John W. *England Before and After Wesley: The Evangelical Revival and Social Reform*. New York: Russell, 1971.

Cambridge Modern History, Volume VI. C.U.P., 1909.

Carter, Henry. *The Methodist Heritage*. Epworth, 1952.

Christie, I. R. *The End of North's Ministry*. Macmillan, 1958.

Davies, R. E. *Methodism*. Pelican, 1963.

Derry, John W. *Reaction and Reform, 1793–1868: England in the Early Nineteenth Century*. Atlantic Highlands, N.J.: Humanities Press, Inc., 1968.

Fisher, H.A.L. *History of Europe*, Vol. II. Eyre and Spottiswoode, 1935.

Green, V.H.H. *The Young Mr. Wesley*. Arnold, 1961.

Harris, Ronald W. *England in the Eighteenth Century, 1689–1793: A Balanced Constitution and New Horizons*. Atlantic Highlands, N.J.: Humanities Press, Inc., 1968.

Knox, R. A. *Enthusiasm*. New York: Oxford University Press, 1950.

Lewis, W. S. *Horace Walpole*. Hart-Davis, 1961.

Lunn, Arnold. *John Wesley*. Cassell, 1929.

Marlow, J. *The Puritan Tradition in British Life*. Cresset, 1957.

Marriott, Sir John. *Oxford*. Oxford University Press, 1933.

Marshall, Dorothy. *English People in the Eighteenth Century*. Longmans, 1956.

Nicolson, Sir Harold. *The Age of Reason*. Constable, 1960.

Overton, J. H. *The Evangelical Revival in the Eighteenth Century*. Longmans, 1886.

Piette, M. *John Wesley in the Evolution of Protestantism*. Sheed and Ward, 1937.

Plumb, J. *Sir Robert Walpole*. Cresset, 1956.

Rattenbury, J. E. *Wesley's Legacy to the World*. Epworth, 1938.

Rowden, A. W. *Primates of the Four Georges*. Murray, 1916.

Todd, John M. *John Wesley and the Catholic Church*. Naperville, Ill.: Alec R. Allenson, Inc., 1958.

Trevelyan, George M. *English Social History*. New York: David McKay Co., Inc., 1965.

Turberville, Arthur S. (editor). *Johnson's England*. New York: Oxford University Press, 1933.

Tyerman, L. *Life and Times of John Wesley*, 3 vols. Hodder and Stoughton, 1872.

Vulliamy, C. E. *John Wesley*, 3rd edition. Epworth, 1954.

Watson, Bishop R. *Anecdotes of Life of,* 2 vols. London, 1818.

Wearmouth, R. F. *The Social-Political Influence of Methodism in the Twentieth Century*. Epworth, 1957.